Five-Star
Basketball
Defense

Five-Star Basketball Defense

Edited by Leigh Klein
with Shay Berry, Tony Bergeron and Kevin Pigott

equilibrium
books
A Division of Wish Publishing

Book edited by Leigh Klein with Shay Berry, Tony Bergeron and Kevin Pigott
Cover designed by Phil Velikan
Editorial assistance provided by Heather Lowhorn, Dorothy Chambers and Adam Parmenter

Printed in the United States of America
10 9 8 7 6 5 4 3 2 1

Published in the United States by
Equilibrium Books, A Division of Wish Publishing
P.O. Box 10337
Terre Haute, Indiana 47801, USA
www.wishpublishing.com

Distributed in the United States by
Cardinal Publishers Group
Indianapolis, Indiana

Table of Contents

Introduction

This book is built by the coaching fraternity. At Five-Star Camp, we have been moved by many of the great coaches that have come through and influenced the game. They have left a legacy of learning and education by sharing their ideas, notes, drills and philosophies with others and have not been afraid to think out of the box.

For the past two years, we at Five-Star Basketball have been working on providing coaches the most comprehensive guide to coaching defense. Basketball continues to evolve every year, and yet many of the greatest philosophies within our game come from the coaching geniuses of the '50s and '60s. Coaching is very much like cooking, where you play with "recipes" of the past and mix in or take out ingredients to come up with something amazing.

Our purpose is to inspire thought and to give both experienced and aspiring coaches the tools, techniques and philosophies that have shaped many great defenses so that you can mold them into a defensive system that matches your personnel and coaching philosophy.

The need to re-emphasize defense is great. With athleticism transforming the modern game, many core defensive fundamentals are not getting the attention that is necessary to allow for player progression and consistency. There is no shortcut to great defense. It requires tireless effort toward individual defensive techniques and team defensive concepts.

Leigh Alan Klein
President, Five-Star Basketball

"Defense is about being coachable." – Hubie Brown

Bernie Holowicki
Madonna College, MI

What People Should Be Saying About Our Basketball Team

- "Man, they play hard."

- "Man, they guard people."

- "Man, they're unselfish."

- "Man, they don't show up anybody."

- "Man, are they a class act on and off the court."

- "Man, I wish we could be like them."

Part One:
Preseason Planning,
Preparation and
Conditioning

Mike Granato
Weir High School, WV

Preseason Planning and the Implementation of Man Defense in High School

Introduction

Preseason planning is a major part of any head coach's responsibility and an important component of successful programs. My experiences in the past 24 years have taught me the value of organization at all levels in our program.

The most difficult thing to teach and organize at the high school level is man-to-man defense. Our philosophy is to play as much man defense as we possibly can. Since it is the most difficult thing to teach, we feel that organization over a long period of time is essential for success. We have developed a defensive philosophy that is based on our man principles. While we do use multiple defenses, our zone packages serve as a change-up for our man defense. A typical season at Weir High School would have us playing 75% to 80% man defense.

Before we plan for our preseason practices, we develop a checklist of what we will cover. Our checklist varies some from season to season. During each preseason, I make a checklist that is based on the man offenses of our opponents. I then compare it to our master checklist (diagram 1). We try to cover all aspects of man defense, whether it is half court or full court, during our preseason. We place special emphasis on our December opponents to keep our principles in the players' minds as best we can. I place a copy of the checklist in the office so that we can mark off when we cover one of our objectives (diagram 2).

All coaches have to decide how they will implement their defensive system. The following questions must be included:

- Do we deny the wing, or do we "shrink the court" to take away the back-door cut?
- How do we play the pick-and-roll? Do we go under? Trap? Switch?
- How do we play the low post? Do we front, side-high, side-low or play behind?
- Do we square up on the offensive player or give a side on the perimeter?
- How far do we extend pressure? When?
- When do we double down on the post? From what angle do we do this?
- Should we switch on screens? When and how?
- Do we force middle or baseline?
- How do we find our man in defensive transition?

There are many more questions that may be asked. It is important that all members of the staff are on the same page as the implementation of our defensive system takes place. Terminology, concepts and philosophy must be consistent throughout all levels. One of the most difficult things facing head coaches at the high school level is making sure that their system is taught correctly in the lower levels. As much as the head coach would like, it is impossible to attend all practices at the lower levels.

Weir Basketball Man Defense Checklist

1. Wing denial–six point drill

2. Play the basket cut–guard to forward pass

3. Screens–one-step cushion to pull the man through

    • Downscreen

    • Post-to-post screen

    • Perimeter ball screens (pick-and-roll)

    • Scissor cut

4. Cut through

5. Cut through off double screen

6. Flex cut

7. Help and recover

    • Perimeter–stop penetration and play square

    • Baseline rotation

        - Baseline post holds

        - Weak-side post rotates over to help

        - Weak-side guard sags

8. Possible switching situations

    • We only switch when necessary

    • Coaches determine switching situations, not players

9. Post defense

    • Guards always front the post on cut through or straight post up

    • Low-post rules

        - Ball above foul line extended–step above denial

        - Ball below foul line extended–side high

        - Ball on baseline–underneath denial or front

        - Play behind the post if not an offensive threat

        - Post-to-post screen–automatic front on switch

        - Jam and deny the flash from opposite low post–force higher

All items should be covered by the first game. The best way to do this is to use the four-on-four shell drill daily.

Diagram 1

WEIR BASKETBALL MAN TO MAN CHECKLIST										
WING DENIAL - 6 PT. DRILL										
JUMP TO THE BALL "BASKET CUT"										
DOWNSCREEN										
BACKSCREEN										
POST TO POST SCREEN - "ACROSS"										
POST TO POST SCREEN - DIAGONAL										
PERIMETER SCREEN - "FLARE"										
PERIMETER SCREEN - PICK AND ROLL										
SCISSOR CUT										
CUT THRU										
CUT THRU OFF DOUBLE SCREEN										
STAGGER SCREEN										
FLEX CUT										
HELP/RECOVER										
BASELINE ROTATION										
WEAKSIDE HELP - MOTION										
DEFEND THE CURL										
DENY THE FLASH POST										
CLOSEOUTS - ON BALL										
CLOSEOUTS - FROM WEAKSIDE										
BACKDOOR CUTS										
POST ISOLATION										

Diagram 2

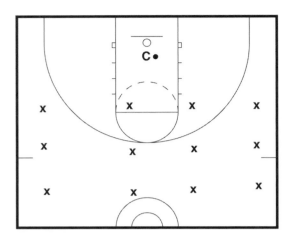

Diagram 3

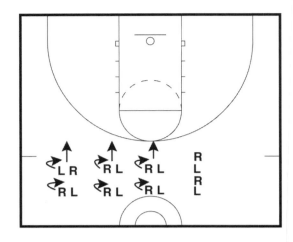

Diagram 4

Implementation

Our junior varsity team normally practices with the varsity squad. This forces us to be very organized in our practice schedule to make sure that all the players are getting enough reps against the right level of competition.

Stretching is very important for teams who are going to be doing defensive drills at the beginning of practice. The lower back and hamstrings have to be loose in order for the player to participate effectively and avoid injury. Our pre-practice sessions usually take 30 to 35 minutes, and we mix offensive and defensive drills. We do each of the following drills on a daily basis to help us defensively:

Team defense

This is the basic defensive stance drill (diagram 3). With a coach in front of the group, place the players in straight lines so that they have room to move. As the coach pulls the ball toward his body, the players yell "advance" and take one slide-step forward. As he pushes the ball away from his body, the players yell "retreat" and take one slide-step back. As the coach dribbles at the players, they open up and slide, using a drop step every time the coach crossover dribbles and changes direction. Once the players are moving, the coach can drop the ball at any time. At the dropping of the ball, the players dive onto the floor. This drill teaches players to never lose sight of the ball.

One-on-one in the full court

This is a simple variation of the zigzag drill. Players guard the ball and turn the dribbler. At midcourt the dribbler stops briefly, and the defender yells "fire" while trapping chest-to-chest. This is the signal that the ball handler has used his dribble (diagram 4).

Three-on-two/two-on-one

This is a variation of every fast-break drill run in basketball. We start with two defenders in the midcourt circle. On the outlet to the guard, the two defenders sprint to the paint with the top man calling "I got ball." The bottom man takes the first pass to the wing. The goal in defensive transition is to get the ball out of the middle as soon as possible. The earlier the ball is thrown to the wing, the easier it is to recover. Once the ball is shot and rebounded by the defense, the two defenders become offensive players. If the shot goes in, one player quickly takes the ball out of bounds and outlets the ball to the side where the wing is. The offense brings the ball down the floor two-on-one with the point guard sprinting back to defend. The goal in the two-on-one situation is to take a charge or force the offense to overpass to get help back in a game situation.

As we finish these drills, we formally start our practice with our four-on-four shell drill in order to work on our defensive fundamentals. We will extend our shell drill to full court when necessary to work on full-court pressure defense. In the preseason we will spend 12 to 15 minutes daily on both ends of the court with both the varsity and junior varsity players working on the same fundamental skills of our man defense. During the season, this time in practice will be used to review our opponent's offense before we put in the live

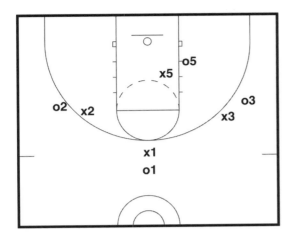

Diagram 5

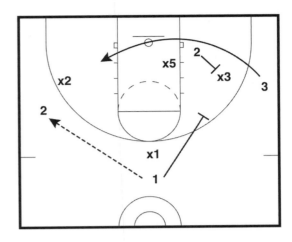

Diagram 6

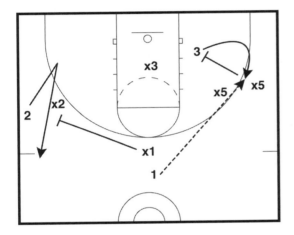

Diagram 7

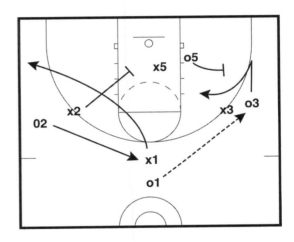

Diagram 8

section of our practice plan. As a staff we review our checklist and begin our teaching progression. It should be noted that our four-on-four shell drill is normally run from a single-guard front with a point guard, two wings and a post (diagram 5). This formation helps us to defend the flex cut (diagram 6), motion sets (diagram 7) and the pick-and-roll (diagram 8). If we are playing a team that runs a Princeton-style of-

fense, we use a traditional box or shell alignment with our opponent's offensive rules. Scouting plays a major role in our defensive planning once the season starts. It should be noted that in all of our defensive drills, one coach would be placed in charge of individual rebounding block outs within the group. We normally place one assistant under the basket to be able to watch the entire floor.

To Take Your Game to the Next Level: Exaggerate your stance and stay as low as possible. This will help you late in games. You want to be able to stay in your stance and shut down your man.

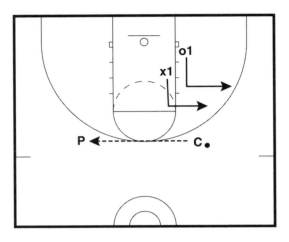

Diagram 9

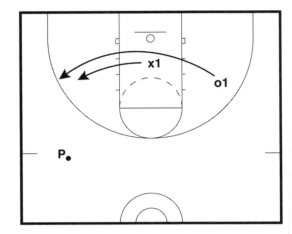

Diagram 10

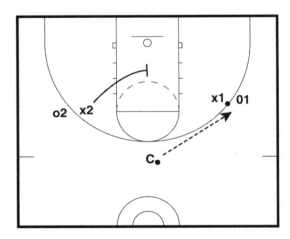

Diagram 11

Man defensive drills also can build mental and physical toughness for the individuals involved. As part of our defensive progression, we believe in doing wing-denial drills either one-on-one or two-on-two with a coach. Regardless of how a coach decides to play his man defense, this drill can be beneficial. We teach our principles of ball-you-man in both situations. In our one-on-one wing denial drill, we will enter the ball to the strong-side wing or reverse it to a passer on the opposite wing (diagrams 9 and 10). On ball reversal, the defender opens up to the ball into the lane and jams the cutter. The ball may then be entered into the wing. Now the wing and his defender play one-on-one. The offensive player gets three dribbles. In our two-on-two drill, the coach plays the point and serves as an outlet once the ball is entered to a wing (diagram 11). Any defensive philosophy can now be served as live play begins.

Mike Feagans
Rensselaer Central High School, NY

Defensive Preseason Preparation

Introduction

When we meet as a staff before the season begins, I want to make sure that our coaches know the defensive priorities we are going to set for the year. Being a high school program, I will explain this philosophy to all the coaches on staff including the feeder programs. We want the entire staff, to share the same attitude. We want to be the best defensive team in the state. The following drills are designed to make our players better defensive players. Great defenders play with great intensity and great desire. That is how these defensive drills must be done. Improving foot speed and lateral movement is very difficult. It can be accomplished with hard work and determination.

Defensive Philosophy

Defense is the most important factor in winning any basketball game. As long as we play outstanding defense, we will always have a chance to win every game. As an individual and a team you must possess the following characteristics to be good defensively:

- Intensity –playing as hard as you can on every possession.
- Pride—in your ability to stop your opponent offensively.
- Desire—to help your team win at all costs.
- Communication—with your teammates.

Even though the following defensive areas are simple, we must constantly push ourselves to achieve at a higher level. We focus on:

- Opponent's field goal percentage
- Defensive stops
- Rebounding
- Loose balls
- Charges
- Shots in the red zone

If we outdo our opponents in these six categories, we will win the majority of our games. These aspects of defense will make or break us.

Breakdown of Successful Defense

To play defense, one must be determined. One must have the attitude of "My man or my teammate's man will not score." Our defensive philosophy must be a five-versus-one instead of one-versus-one. Players in our program must always know where the ball is and where their man is located. Defenders must always communicate with each other about the location of the ball and screens. The purpose of defense is simple—to stop the other team from scoring.

Defensive Rules

1. Stance
   - Bend with buttocks down and head up. Spread your chest.
   - Arm bar—one hand in the passing lane.
   - Have your feet pointed directly at your opponent's feet.
2. Always pressure the ball.
3. If our opponent stops their dribble and picks up the ball, get all over the offensive player with arms straight up. Stay on your feet.
4. Always move while the ball is in the air.
5. Don't try to steal the ball. Move with your feet to the spot that the offense is going to.
6. Force the dribbler to go to the weak hand.
7. Challenge all shots with an approach step.
8. When your man does not have the ball, form a triangle between your man and the ball, i.e., get in a ball-you-man position.
9. Always be on the help side if your man does not have the ball.

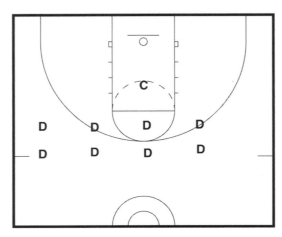

Diagram 12

Diagram 13

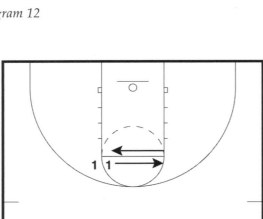

Diagram 14

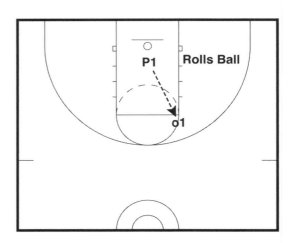

Diagram 15

10. Build an attitude on defense, i.e., "You are not going to score on me!"

Drills for Improving Individual Defense

Jump rope
Spend about five to 10 minutes a day jumping rope. Use one foot, then two feet. Alternate footwork.

Stance Drill (diagram 12)
Start by slapping the floor and assuming a good defensive position. Knees should be bent, hands active, back straight with heels off the ground. Begin by holding this position for 30 seconds. Gradually increase the time until you can hold your stance for two minutes.

Rim jumps (diagram 13)
We make our players jump and touch the rim or backboard for 30 seconds. It is a repeat jump; as soon as you hit the floor, you bounce right back up.

Foot fire drill
Begin by slapping the floor and assuming a good defensive stance. Quickly move feet up and down while staying in your stance. Continue the drill for 30 seconds. Slowly build until you can go for two minutes. Break up the drill by adding quarter turns left and right. These turns should be done as quickly as possible with feet touching down and then returning to the original position.

Lateral slides (diagram 14)
Begin in a good defensive stance with both feet outside the lane. Slide across the lane as quickly

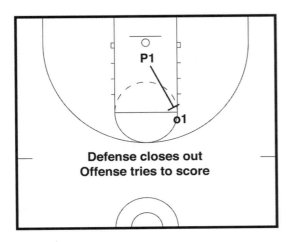

Diagram 16

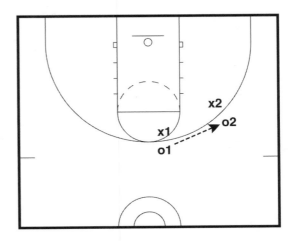

Diagram 17

as possible while maintaining good defensive position. When moving to the left, point the left foot 90 degrees left and push off with the right foot. Reverse this movement as you move to the right. You should push and slide, not letting your feet come together. Slide until both feet are outside the lane and then return, working to keep your head level. Do not bob up and down as you slide.

Go for 30 seconds and look to improve your total with each workout.

Bomber drill (diagram 15)

The defensive player roles the ball to the offensive player at elbow. The offensive player gets in a triple-threat position or takes the ball directly to the hoop upon collecting the ball. If the offensive player gets into the triple-threat position, he can use a variety of moves (e.g., jab, crossover, rocker, shot fake).

The defensive player closes out on offensive player and attempts to stop the offensive player. The defensive player must use a quick first step after getting in hisstance (diagram 16).

The coach can dictate the number of dribbles available to the offensive player.

Two-on-two with jump to the ball (diagram 17)

Point passes to the wing. The wing defender quickly jumps to the offensive wing and gets in a defensive stance. The point defender jumps to the ball and plays his position one-pass-away.

Remember to stay in your stance. The drill can become live upon coach's command.

Joe Stolzer
Five-Star Basketball Camp

Conditioning: Strength and Speed Workout

In today's game, defense is all about getting to a spot. How quick are you? In today's game, 31% of all movement is lateral. Why don't we train that way? The fastest player is the one whose feet rest are the floor for the shortest period of time. When conditioning, remember—you must strengthen your weak areas.

Warm-Up

When warming up, your goal is to raise your body temperature by two degrees. Exercise lightly for 10 minutes using any of the following exercises:

- *Skipping*
- *Jogging forward and backward*
- *Jumping rope*
- *Jumping jacks*
- *Running backward:* This creates a balance in your front and back muscles.
- *Slide-shuffles:* Assume a defensive stance. Work on proper positioning of hands and feet. Do not focus on speed. That will come with practice.
- *Lunges:* Perform the lunges with 45 degrees to the right or left.
- *Squat thrusts*

Lateral Movement

Perform at defensive speed.

- *Line touches:* Do 30 in 30 seconds, 40 in 40 seconds, etc.
- *Basketball volley:* Have the player slide across lane while a partner tosses him a tennis ball. The player catches the ball with one hand and tosses it back.
- *Lateral hurdles:* Lay three hurdles on their side on the ground. The player must move across them in a line by jumping side-to-side.
- *Boxing:* Have the player jump on and off the board, scissoring feet and throwing punches.

Vertical Jump

The vertical jump is a measure of one's true explosive power.

- *Pogo jumps:* Do 20 short, 20 high.
- *Broad jump:* Jump off two feet; jump forward as far as you can.
- *Overspeed:* Sprint from half-court to baseline coming to a jump stop before jumping as high as you can. Try to touch the backboard with both hands.
- *Knees to chest/heels to butt:* Do three sets of 25 reps. Jump with the goal of bringing your knees to the level of your chest.

Reaction Time

- *Reaction time exercise:* Get with a partner and jump on the ball release, on the bounce of a ball, on the sound of a whistle, on hand claps or on flash of fingers (e.g., only jumping on three fingers up).

Agility

- *Agility exercise:* Change directions and keep speed up. Start in a corner of the court and sprint to the opposite diagonal corner. Slide across the baseline. Sprint to the opposite diagonal corner. Slide across the baseline and finish where you started.
- *Change of speed:* Jog, run and sprint. Keep it game-like by changing the speed.

Foot and Ankle

Foot and ankle strength affects knee stability and hip strength. Often a bad knee is the result of a weakness in the foot and ankle areas.

- *Foot and ankle exercise:* Walk on toes for one minute. Walk on heels for one minute. Jog barefoot in place for five to 15 minutes.
- *Side ankle lifts:* Lie on your side with a partner standing above you. Push your ankle upward. As you push upward your partner creates resistance by pushing down on your foot.
- *Toe-ups:* Lift your toes upward. Do 30 reps.

Legs

Basketball is played from one leg to the other. A major key of basketball strength is the ability to transfer weight from one leg to the other.

- *One leg get-up:* Standing with your back to a bench, raise one foot barely off the ground and lower your body to sit on the bench. Do 10 reps, then switch legs.
- *Iso explosion:* Squat on one leg, hold for four seconds, then jump as high as you can.
- *One leg squat:* Standing on a bench, squat on one leg. Hold for 30 seconds. Do exercise for five minutes.
- *Train on one leg:* Jump from side to side, then hold for four seconds. Jump from front to back, then hold for four seconds.
- *Jumps:* Jump 1-2-3 front to back using both legs. Jump 1-2-3 left to right using both legs.

Pillar Strength

The emphasis should be on inner abs rather than outer abs. No matter how big an athlete is, on the court he is only as strong as his inner abs.

- *Planks:* This is a top ab exercise for everyone from soccer moms to Kobe Bryant.
- *Bridge:* Lying on your back with your shoulders and feet on the ground, raise the body from the tailbone to the neck and hold for 30 seconds. Over time, try and hold for progressively longer periods of time, up to five minutes. This strengthens the body in a synergistic way.
- *Figure-eight:* Sitting with your buttocks on the ground and your legs as straight as possible and raised, wrap the ball around and through your legs in a figure-eight motion while moving your legs up and down. Go 30 seconds to one minute. This improves hand-eye coordination, basketball-specific muscles, shoulders, core and hips.
- *Bicycle lateral raises:* Sitting on a chair, move your legs in a bicycle motion while performing lateral raises with 10 pound weights.

Upper Body Strength

- *Squat thrust into a push-up into a vertical jump:* Do 20 reps with a 20-second rest. Do 19 reps with a 19-second rest. Continue the sequence down to one.
- *Dips:* Hang between two chairs with one hand on each chair and bend at the elbow to dip between the two chairs. Work up to 50 reps.

Hands

- *Ball push-ps:* Roll the ball from one hand to the other.
- *Quick hands:* Throw the ball up. Clap eight to 10 times before catching it.
- *Touch the stove:* Use your imagination and pretend to touch a hot stove. When you touch a hot stove, you would quickly move your hand away, like an explosion. Practice touching the hot stove, have your hand explode away from it.

Gluteus Medius

- *Coach hang:* Lie down sideways on the bench, rest the bottom leg on bench on your ankle.

Back

- *Kneeling outlet pass:* Kneeling on the floor, throw outlet passes to a partner. Your partner will move back a few paces on each set of 10 passes.

Areas of Concern

- In the 60 minutes after a workout your body is peaking. It is then that you must replenish the nutrients.
- The taller the player is, the longer his spine is, thus the greater the need for muscle development to protect the spine.

- Hamstrings are important to a strong vertical jump, but they are the weakest muscles in the lower body.

- The glutes give you 80% of your vertical jump. Make sure they are strong.

- To strengthen the lower back and the front of the calf, run backward for four minutes.

Part Two:
Individual Defense

Tony Bergeron
Five-Star Basketball Camp
East Longmeadow High School, MA

Teaching Defensive Stance

Proper Defensive Stance

It is impossible to play defense if you are not balanced and if you do not understand defensive stance. In every single practice we constantly work on stance, balance, footwork and body control. In proper defensive stance, you want your feet just underneath the armpits. The back is straight. The backside is low, and the knees are bent. We want to keep our hands out wide to our sides. Some coaches teach their players to keep one hand up and one hand down. We have found that this could cause players to be unbalanced. We want our players to be strong in the trunk but loose up top. By being flexed on top you cannot be knocked off balance. Your feet are flat on the floor. You are not on the balls of your feet. From heel to toe you are touching the floor. Keep feet flat for lateral movement.

Step slide

Point the toe of your lead foot while you step slide. By pointing the toe, you will not roll the ankle when you change direction. This also allows you to change direction quickly. As you step with the lead foot you will use the inside of the rear foot and slide quickly in the same direction. As you move, your heals do not come together. They actually get farther apart. Stay in good defensive stance throughout the movement.

Angle slide

In this day and age of ultra-gifted athletes, you have to work on more than balance, stance and lateral movement in order to effectively guard a ball handler. To stop some of the more gifted athletes today, players have to work on angling their bodies and picking spots ahead. Aggressively lead with the elbow to angle the body, then step slide into position.

Kevin Pigott
Fordham Preparatory School, NY

Defensive Stance Drills

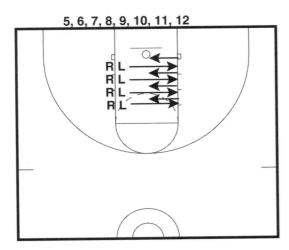

5, 6, 7, 8, 9, 10, 11, 12

Diagram 18

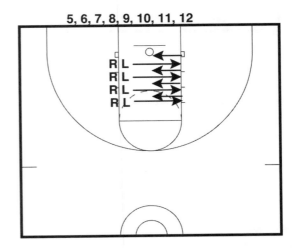

5, 6, 7, 8, 9, 10, 11, 12

Diagram 19

The most important skill for the defensive player is his stance. We spend a great amount of time in developing our stance. The following are some of the drills we use to improve our defensive stance.

Stance and transition drill

Line four players on the side of the paint area facing down court. Line eight more players on the baseline. Rotation consists of three groups, each consisting of four players (diagram 18). Each player in the first group has his right foot outside paint, his left foot in paint. On the coach's command of "stance," players slap the floor with their palms, yell "defense," and slide to the side (diagram 19). On the coach's command of "break," the first group sprints to the opposite baseline or to half court. The second group replaces the first group. The first group jogs up the sideline to the starting spot.

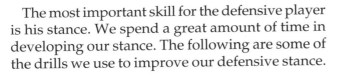

To Take Your Game to the Next Level: No matter whether you are guarding the ball, denying one-pass-away, or even in the paint playing help-side defense, your lower trunk motion should be the same.

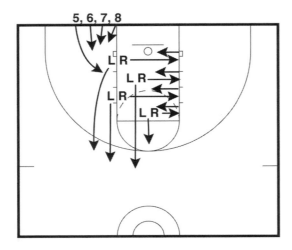

Diagram 20

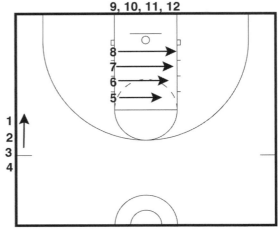

Diagram 21

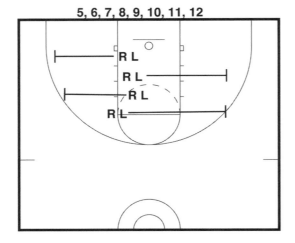

Diagram 22

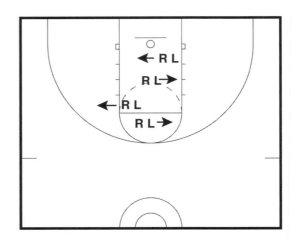

Diagram 23

The last player of the second group yells "stance" when they are ready. All players get in their stance, slap the floor and yell "defense" (diagram 20). The second group slides until the coach yells "break." The first group comes back on the sideline at half speed. The third group waits in line for their turn in the rotation to replace second group (diagram 21).

Stance and close-out drill

Players line up as they did before (diagram 18). On the coach's command of "stance," players slap the floor with their palms, yell "defense," and slide to the side (diagram 19). On the coach's command of "close out," the first and third players will close out to their left. The second and fourth players close out to their right (diagram 22). The second

group replaces the first group. Continue the rotation with the third group.

Stance and dive drill

Players line up as they did before (diagram 18). On the coach's command of "stance," players slap the floor with their palms, yell "defense," and slide to side (diagram 19). On the coach's command of "dive," the first and third players will dive to their left to retrieve an imaginary loose ball. The second and fourth players will dive to their right to retrieve an imaginary loose ball (diagram 23). The second group replaces the first group. Continue the rotation with the third group.

Stance and one-pass-away drill

The players line up with two players at the elbows and two players on the blocks. At the coach's

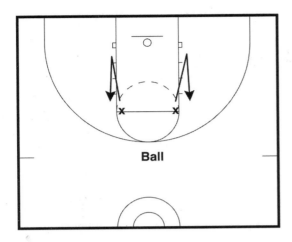

Diagram 24

Diagram 25

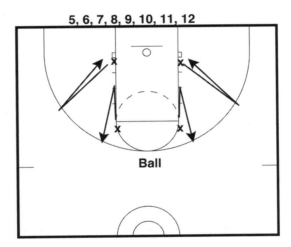

Diagram 26

command, the players at the elbows will continually move from the elbow to the block back to the elbow. They will simulate a denial defensive position as if the ball was at the top of the key and they were denying the post flash (diagram 24).

At the coach's command, the players at the blocks will continually move from the block to the wing and back to the block. They will simulate a denial defensive position, as if the ball was at the top of the key and they were denying the wing (diagram 25).

All four players can now go at once upon the coach's command. The next command by the coach will be "break," in which all four players sprint to either the opposite baseline or half-court and then jog back up the sideline to the original baseline. The second group replaces the first group. The third group waits in line (diagram 26).

Stance and box-out drill

We do this drill as part of our sequence of stance drills. It certainly helps us in learning to box out. You can find this drill in the chapter on man-to-man defense.

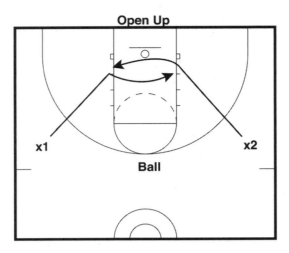

Diagram 27

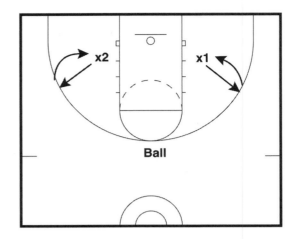

Diagram 28

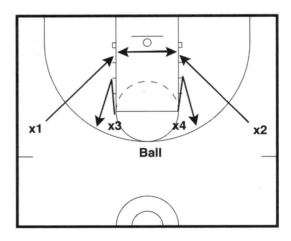

Diagram 29

To Take Your Game to the Next Level: Players should rotate wing and elbow positions. You can have your wing players open up as they get to the block and then slide across to the other block. These players must communicate or there will be collisions (diagram 27 and 28). Remember, this is going on while the two other players are moving from elbow to block to elbow (diagram 29).

Multipurpose Lane Slides

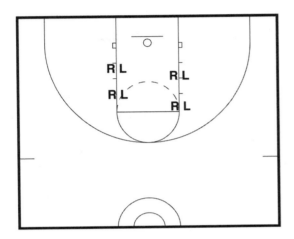

Diagram 30

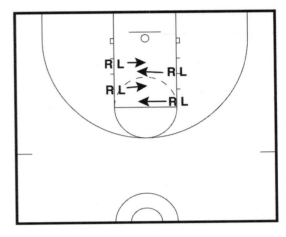

Diagram 31

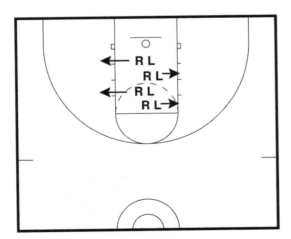

Diagram 32

We like this drill not only because it involves different defensive skills, but also because it allows the coach to control the pace. This drill teaches stance, close outs, contesting and boxing out. We can also use it as a conditioning drill. It also gives our players the opportunity to work on their communication skills and peripheral vision.

Players will line up on the sides of the three-second lane (diagram 30). On the coach's command of "one in," each player will take one step toward the middle. If the command is "two in," each player will take two steps in (diagram 31). The coach will use the commands of "one out" or "two out" to move the players back outside the paint (diagram 32).

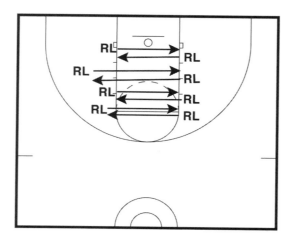

Diagram 33

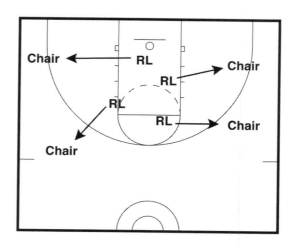

Diagram 34

The command "cross" will get the players to move continually from one side of the paint to the other. Each player must get both feet outside the paint before he can change direction (diagram 33). Players must have faith in their peripheral vision; they must look ahead and not look to their sides. They also must communicate with each other in order to avoid collisions.

N.B.:

On the coach's command of "close out," the player will close out to an imaginary offensive player. We use a chair to simulate this offensive player (diagram 34). After they close out, the players will get in a good defensive stance. In the close out we want our players to move quickly but stay low. When they get near the offensive player, i.e., the chair, they will shuffle their feet in order to get in a good defensive stance.

The coach will use the command "contest" to simulate a shot by the offensive player. The player will now contest the shot without leaving his feet. On the command "box," the player will box out the offensive player. The coach will designate before the drill which type of pivot he wants the defender to use.

This drill can be done at different paces. We can make it competitive by using live offensive players instead of chairs. We can keep the pace slow in order to teach footwork. This will work well with lower level teams.

To Take Your Game to the Next Level: Players must be in a good defensive stance. Their feet should be shoulder-width apart, and their base should be low. We tell the players to "sit down." In this drill we keep our hands high and wide. This position gives us balance and allows us to feel and see our sides. Our lead foot is pointed 45 degrees in the direction we are moving. We slide the lead foot. The rear foot pushes us in the direction we are going. We must keep our feet away from each other by taking short, quick steps.

Post Defense

Picture 1

Picture 2

Picture 3

Ball at Point/Top of Key

The post defender must have active feet and stay low in his stance. Deny the ball with your top hand. The other hand is up and off the offensive player. Do not lean on the offensive player. Defend the high side. Stop the ball with your top hand. Split the offensive player's body with your legs. See the ball. Use your peripheral vision. Be in a ball-you-man position (picture 1).

Ball Moves From Point to Wing

Swim through and get his hands up. Front the ball. Be in athletic position with the knees bent. Your arms are up over head (picture 2).

Ball Moves From Wing to Corner

Take one step to the baseline by dropping the inside foot (picture 3). Your feet are now parallel to the baseline with your butt facing the baseline. Deny with the lead hand. Deny ball entry. Take away the pass. Split the offensive player's body. Do not be too high or else the offensive player will seal you off on ball reversal (picture 4).

Picture 4

Picture 5

Picture 6

Picture 7

Picture 8

If Entry Pass is Made

Sink behind the offensive player. Step to the inside (picture 5). Stop penetration. Contest the shot. Stay low in a defensive stance. Box out on the shot.

Ball Moves From Point to Corner on Skip Pass

Go underneath the offensive player. Get in position, denying the ball with your lead hand. Your butt is facing the baseline. Do not swim through and front the ball. Go underneath. This will prevent the offensive player from sealing off the post defender and ducking in on the skip pass (picture 6).

Help and Recover on Penetration From a Guard

The post defender must see and recognize guard penetration. The post defender opens up and helps (picture 7). The post defender then recovers to offensive post man.

Defending the High Post

Most times the high post player is a passer in an offense that involves UCLA or scissor cuts. The post defender plays behind. The post defender looks to play help defense. If our scouting report indicates that the high post player is a good shooter, we will then side front. We will overplay the offensive player's strong hand, i.e., if he is right handed we will deny his right hand. If the ball is on the wing, we will side front the high post facing the ball (picture 8).

Defending the Post

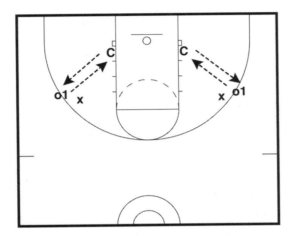

Diagram 35

This drill teaches players how to defend the post from the wing, provides practice for the double, hey fake, butt baseline and substituting techniques and explains terminology for defending the post.

The coach and the offense practice passing back and forth while varying the command for the defensive technique (double, hey fake, etc.) to get repetitions in.

Danny Walck
Reading High School, PA

Man-to-Man Defensive Fundamentals

Prerequisites for Defense

In order for a young athlete to be a great defender, he has to bring the proper attitude to the game. Related to that is a very important question I ask my players: "Are you coachable?" That is the big answer that they have to give to themselves, to me, and to their teammates. The player who is coachable has big things waiting for him. Being coachable means being positive and being focused. The coachable player is always thinking about what is best for the team. I cannot emphasize enough the power of being positive and focused.

The stance of the defensive player on the ball
Are you balanced?
- If your feet are parallel, you will be unbalanced.
- Your feet should be staggered. The heel of one foot should be parallel to the toe of the other.
- Your feet must be slightly wider than shoulder-width apart to maintain balance.
- The defensive player wants to be influential, whether he fans or funnels the offensive player. That decision of either fanning to the sideline or funneling to the middle will be made by the coaching staff's defensive philosophy. A staggered stance allows us to force the ball in either direction.

The zone
In order to play defense successfully, you must be in "the zone." You must be in the best possible physical shape. You must condition and develop your hamstrings, quads and abs. Part of being in the zone is the ability to focus and concentrate. The player must be able to transition mentally from offense to defense.

Step and slide
Lateral slides—left and right. Be in the defensive stance as if playing the ball. Your feet should be staggered. Your feet should be just a little longer than shoulder width. When you move to your left, your left foot steps out. Point the left foot to the left. Do not kick the left foot out and overreach. The right foot follows and slides. The right foot comes into the shoulder. The right foot should not touch the left foot. Do the opposite to go right.

To Take Your Game to the Next Level: In practice we will yell "stance" at any time. When the command "stance" is given, all players must get into a defensive stance as if they were guarding the ball and yell "ball." This is a great way to practice the mental transition from offense to defense.

To Take Your Game to the Next Level:

• Some players will try to slide the left foot and step with the right when going to the left. This will make the defender awkward.

• Players must stay low in stance from slide to retreat to recovery. Building up "the zone" allows defenders to stay low in their stance throughout a game.

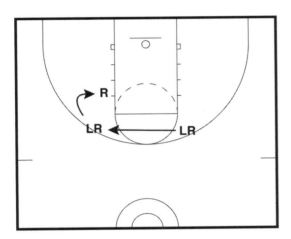

Diagram 36

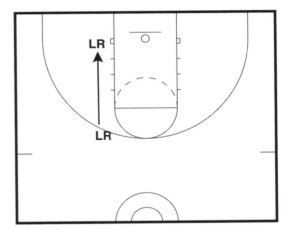

Diagram 37

Retreat and recovery step

While moving to your right laterally, stop and drop the right foot (diagram 36). To retreat, step and slide using your bottom foot to step and your top foot to slide. In this case, your right foot steps and your left foot slides (diagram 37). To recover, drop your left foot. You will be back in your stance (diagram 38).

Hands

Have active hands. Keep your arms wide. Keep your hands off the offensive player–no fouls. Fouling negates good defense.

Step-and-slide drill with retreat and recover

Players are in a defensive stance as if playing on the ball.

On the coach's command of "slide," step and slide to the direction the coach is pointing. Take two steps. When you finish with the two steps, yell "ball."

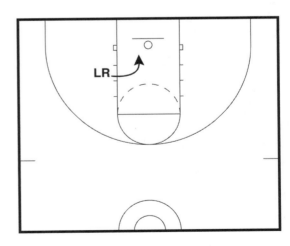

Diagram 38

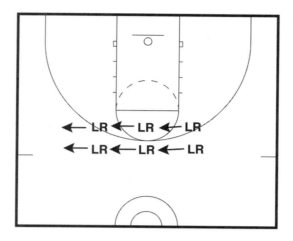

Diagram 39

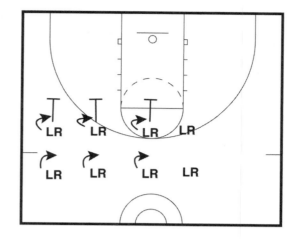

Diagram 40

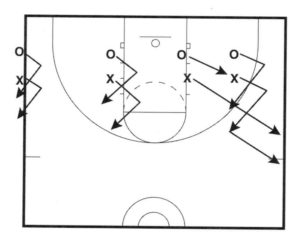

Diagram 41

Follow the coaches commands. The coach's commands consist of "slide," "retreat," "recover" and "relax."

- Start in stance—players get in balanced defensive position.
- Step (diagram 39). The step command can be given as "step left" or "step right" or the coach can point in the direction they want the players to go.
- Retreat (diagram 40)
- Recover (diagram 41)
- Relax – players get out of stance and take a break.

Close out

When we close out, we will fan the offense, i.e., we will channel the ball to the baseline midpoint area. In their desire to hustle, defenders will some-times make one of the following three mistakes while closing out:

- Run by the offensive player
- Foul the offensive player
- Stand up and get out of stance.

You want to challenge the shot. Do not jump at the offensive player. However, when you reach him, get in his numbers. Get big and challenge the shot vertically. Do not long jump to reach the offensive player but high jump to challenge the shot. Challenge the shooter with one foot up on him. The defensive player has to go hard but be under control while closing out and challenging the shot.

Close-out slide drill

You can add the close-out technique to the step-and-slide drill from above. The footwork for the

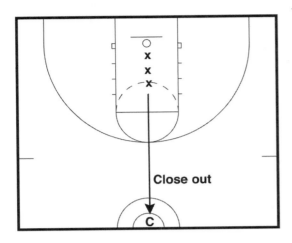

Diagram 42

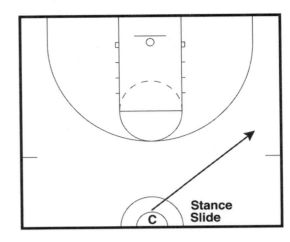

Diagram 43

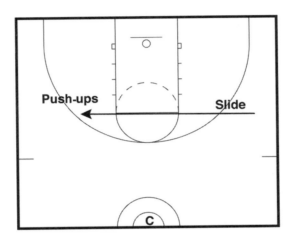

Diagram 44

close out would be the opposite of retreat step. On the coach's command of "close out," the defenders slide up and then get big to challenge the shot. You want to influence the path of the ball handler. Don't allow the offensive player a straight path.

Fan your man drill

This is also known as the defensive force slide drill. Players close out to half-court area (diagram 42). Players slide to sideline foul.line extended (diagram 43). Players slide through to the opposite foul line extended where they do two push-ups (diagram 44). The players go back to the baseline to continue the drill.

Coach has the ball at half court. In order to teach ball-you-man, the coach can throw the ball to any player. The receiver of the pass must pass the ball right back to the coach even if he is moving. Dur-

ing this drill, technique usually breaks down. This drill brings out old habits. Players get out of stance and stop talking. Players must focus and stay low in stance.

Tracing the ball

Because of our great defensive pressure on the ball and the proper footwork in our slides, we cause the ball handler to turn his shoulder to lose his court vision. We want to take away any straight path to the basket. Do not allow the ball handler to drive in straight lines. We have discussed stance and slides. The next part of the progression is tracing the ball. The moment your opponent picks up his dribble, get into him, get up on him, and crossface him.

Use high hands across the offensive player's face when playing a team that is taught to rip the ball through high. Use the crossface technique.

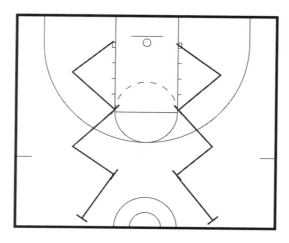

Diagram 45

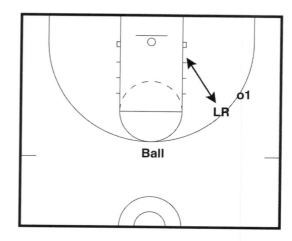

Diagram 46

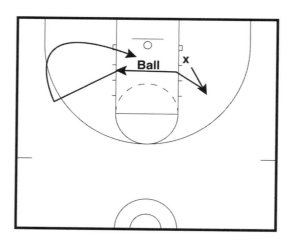

Diagram 47

Use one hand on the ball when playing a team that rips low to high to low. Footwork is important. Move your feet. Move with the offensive player when the ball is ripped. Don't reach. Remember, his dribble is dead.

Tracing the ball drill

Players pair with a partner, one player on defense and one on offense. The coach will yell "stance." On that command, defenders get in stance and yell "ball." The first time through, the offense rips the ball high as defenders use the crossface technique. The second time through, the offense rips low to high to low as the defense traces the ball with one hand.

Zigzag drill

We can glue all the above together with the old-fashioned zigzag drill. Break into pairs. Two pairs will go at once, one pair on the left and the other on the right. The offensive player dribbles from the sideline to the beginning of the three-second area. Go to half court (diagram 45). The defender attempts to turn the dribbler. The defender must beat the offensive player to the spot. The defense must influence the dribbler and shut him down for five seconds. The defense must have the offense pick up his dribble and cause a dead-dribble situation. The defense must trace the ball with either the crossface technique or with one hand on the ball for five seconds. The defense yells "ball." Sprint back to the baseline. The offense goes to defense; defense goes to offense.

Off the ball defense

This drill will work on denying the perimeter pass and opening up in the help side. The footwork and movement is the same whether you are on the ball, defending one-pass-away, or in the help side. The upper torso of the defender one-pass-away does differ, however. The defender will have one hand in the passing lane with his palm facing the ball and his fingers closed. The inside hand will be parallel to the defender's chest to prevent him from holding the offensive player (diagram 46). Remember: Closed fingers prevent jammed fingers.

The ball is on top with the coach. Contest the ball to the three-point arc. Slide up to the arc. Slide back to the paint. The player sliding up to the arc will be underneath the player sliding back to the paint. Players must communicate loudly and use peripheral vision in order to avoid collisions.

Open up in the paint and slide across. Close stance and slide out to the three-point arc. Run around the sideline and go back to the baseline to start drill again (diagram 47). The coach can throw the ball to the player. The player must catch and throw it right back.

An Approach to Defensive Rebounding

Picture 1

There are four keys to good defensive rebounding. First, you have to develop your athletic ability. Second, you must develop your hands. You need great hands! Next, you must learn the art of tipping. Finally, you must learn to box out.

Develop Your Athletic Ability

Vertical jump
- Practice everyday
- Quick bounce—your legs must be "bouncy"

Trampoline drill (picture 1)

Stand in a flexed, athletic position with your hands above your head. Using both legs, jump as high as you can, reaching for the sky. Land on both legs and quickly jump again. Pretend you are bouncing off a trampoline. Your goal is to do two sets of 250 jumps each. Stretch your hamstrings and quads right after the drill.

To Take Your Game to the Next Level: You can make both the self-tip drill and the two-tips drill competitive by adding an offensive player. You can also emphasize boxing out.

Picture 2A

Picture 2B

Superman drill (pictures 2A and 2B)

This is a well-known drill. We use it with the NBA players we train. We want to teach our players how to chase down the rebound, especially after they box out the offensive player. We want to get out-of-area rebounds, not just rebounds that come to us. This skill distinguishes the great rebounder from the good rebounder.

Start outside the lane, i.e., the paint area. Throw the ball high off the backboard. Chase the ball and end outside the lane on the other side. Make sure you rebound while you are in the air. Get the rebound and immediately focus on the next repetition. As you land, immediately get in a flexed athletic position to start the next repetition. Try 20 reps.

Picture 3

Superman drill with partner (picture 3)

Line up as you did for the Superman drill. Place yourself between the basket and your partner. The coach will throw the ball up on the glass. Box out your partner and then chase the ball down as you did in the Superman drill. Chase the ball even if the rebound lands on the floor. It still counts as a rebound. After you rebound and land, hand the ball to the coach and get in a flexed athletic position ready to continue the drill.

Develop Your Hands

Great rebounders have great hands!

One-hand passing drill

Stand 10 to 15 feet from your partner. Using only your left hand, pass the ball to your partner's right hand. Pass and catch using only your left hand. Your partner will pass and catch using only his right hand. Both of you will throw a baseball pass. Use your fingerpads to catch and control the ball.

Switch hands. Using only your right hand, pass the ball to your partner's left hand. Use only one hand to pass and catch the ball. Use your fingerpads to catch and control the ball.

Line up on the baseline with your partner, keeping your spacing. Facing your partner in a defensive stance, slide to half court and then back to the baseline. While you are sliding, pass and catch the ball as you did above using only one hand. Continue the drill using your other hand.

You can do both the stationary and moving versions of this drill using two balls. You can also do a variation of this drill while both stationary and moving. Pass with your left hand while catching with your right hand. Your partner will pass with his left and catch with his right. Switch passing

Picture 4

Picture 5A

hands from left to right. This can be done moving. This drill helps you practice transferring the ball from one hand to the other.

Extended one-hand passing drill

Two players position themselves like the stationary one-hand passing drill. With the right hand, pass to your partner's left hand. Pass just away from your partner's left hand, causing him to jump for the ball. Throw the ball just wide enough to make your partner move his feet (picture 4). Your partner must catch with his left hand only. Once he catches the ball, he must slap it into his right hand. Alternate hands. Do this drill 90 seconds a day.

The purpose of this drill is twofold. First, it teaches the player to chase the ball. Second, it teaches the player to quickly bring the ball to his core strength area.

Learning the Art of Tipping

It does not matter whether you are on defense or offense, great rebounders look for opportunities to the tip ball to themselves. Tipping the rebound to yourself is done when the defensive rebounder is undersized or the defensive rebounder is out of position.

Technique
- Tip the ball away from the offensive player when rebounding in traffic.
- Tip the ball away from the basket toward the ball-side sideline.
- Use the inside arm.
- Extend the arm fully.

Picture 5B

- Use your finger pads.
- The palm of the tipping hand should be facing the sideline.
- Tip the ball high.
- Like any other rebound, chase the ball down. Finish strong.
- Finish with a jump stop.
- Protect the ball.

Backboard tip drill

Throw the ball off the backboard. First use the outside hand. On the right side, tip the ball with the right hand. On the left side, tip the ball with the left hand. Next use the inside hand. On the right side, tip the ball with the left hand. On the left side, tip the ball with the right hand. We use this drill as part of our prestretching.

Self tip drill (picture 5A+B)

Line up on the right side of basket, halfway between the backboard and the foul line. Throw the ball off the backboard. Tip toward the sideline using the inside, i.e. the left hand. Tip high and tip long. Chase the ball down and rebound. Then the next player in line goes. Line up on the left side of the basket and tip with the right hand. Continue the drill.

Two tips drill

Another skill you need to learn is how to tip the rebound more than once. This drill helps teach that. Set the drill up as you did for the self tip drill. After the first tip, tip again with the same hand. On the third touch, rebound the ball.

Learning the Art of the Defensive Box-Out

On the shot, turn and locate your man. Read the shooter. Make contact as the ball is being released by the shooter, not when the ball is in the air. Create contact with your hip and butt. Stay low and get a wide base. Make sure you are in a flexed position with your knees bent.

Hit your man first before he hits you. Many an offensive rebounder will stop upon being hit. Release from your man and attack the ball as it comes off the rim. Rebound and bring the ball to your core strength area. Come down with a jump stop.

Part Three:
Man-to-Man
Team Defense

Hubie Brown
NBA Analyst for TNT
Naismith Basketball Hall of Fame

Teaching Man Defense

What is your defensive philosophy? Are you going to funnel the ball to the middle of the floor, or are you going to fan the ball out to the side? You have to decide what you want to do—funnel or fan. For now, we will look at fanning.

Defensive Commandments

Do not allow the ball to the middle. When the ball is on the wing, force it to the baseline midpoint. The baseline midpoint is a low percentage shot. Play up on the offensive player's leg, splitting him in half. Your shoulders should be squared to the sideline. Go to the midpoint area (diagram 48).

Never foul a jump shooter. If he is having a good night shooting, he will make 50% of his shots. If he is having a good night at the foul line, he will make 80% of his free throws.

Always challenge the shot and block out. You must be at least three feet away on your challenge. Block out with elbows out. By keeping your arms up and elbows out, you make yourself bigger. The offensive player cannot come over the top, and you don't have to turn your head to see him.

Closing out on the Wing

Run at the wing and touch. Run at his chest. Once you reach him, your outside leg will be high. Your inside leg will split the wing in half. Touch him with your right hand (diagram 49).

Touch the wing. You are three feet away. Do not let him shoot a three-point shot. Send the wing to the baseline midpoint area. Do not let him go to the middle.

Do not leave your feet on the ball fake. Elevate only when the wing leaves his feet. If you go for the fake:

- The wing can go inside of you.
- The wing can step over and shoot a three-point shot.
- Challenge the wing's shot. Pivot and block out.

One-on-one drill

Play for two minutes (diagram 50). The defender starts underneath the basket. He throws the ball to the offensive player at the foul line. The defender must be careful not to throw a quick pass

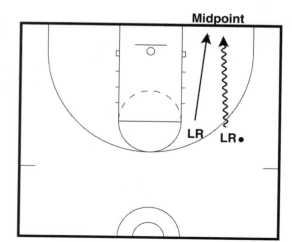

Diagram 48

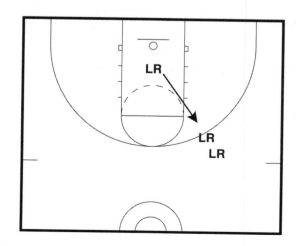

Diagram 49

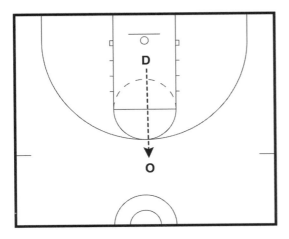

Diagram 50

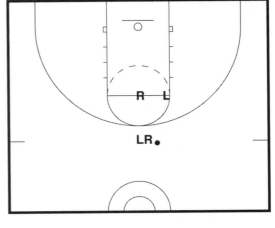

Diagram 51

to the offensive player. If the pass is too quick, the offensive player will have an open shot.

The defense must:

- Challenge the shot.
- Step to the shooter.
- Block out.

Since the ball is in the middle, the defender must split the offensive player's legs on the offensive player's strong side. In this example, we will defend the right-handed player (diagram 51).

The offense gets two dribbles. The offense learns to use the dribble wisely and to penetrate. The offense must pivot well to be successful in this drill.

The offense keeps the ball if they score. If the defense stops the offense, the defense becomes offense. If the offense rebounds, they will try to score. If the defense does not challenge the shot, step to the shooter and block out. The ball goes back to the offense even if the defense gains possession of it.

Statistics

The following are our key statistics in regards to defense. They tell us how aggressive our defense is. We tell our team during every time-out how they are doing with these statistics. Every halftime these statistics go on the board. At the

To Take Your Game to the Next Level, Remember:

- You cannot win at any level unless you can rebound. Defense is aggressiveness. The following drills are built upon intimidation and aggressiveness.
- Touching the offensive player places the defender three feet away from the offensive player. Although it is illegal and might be called a foul during the game, by emphasizing it in practice we instill the habit of being up close to the offensive player with the ball. We want the hand that is on the offensive player to have the palm facing up. This gives the defender the ability to bring his hand up and knock the ball loose. Referees tend not to call the foul when the hand is moving up instead of down on the ball.
- Very seldom do offensive players shoot well while being defended at the baseline midpoint area.
- Great defensive teams challenge every shot.

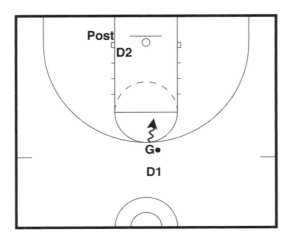

Diagram 52

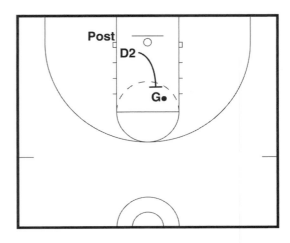

Diagram 53

end of the night these statistics are on the board to remind our players to be aggressive.

- How many turnovers do we force?
- How many steals do we get?
- How many charges and blocked shots do we get?
- How many deflections do we get?

If your man beats you off the dribble, you should not give up. Instead you should chase him into the trap, trying to get a deflection from behind. We want our players to be aggressive and not give up on the ball.

If you are defending your man who is one pass away from the ball, you want to get your inside hand up and attempt to deflect the pass. Deflections are as important as steals, blocked shots and charges.

Deflection drill

You can use three or four players for this drill. There will be a guard with the ball at the top of the key. There is one defender with him. However, the defender has been beaten and is now chasing the ball for a possible deflection. There is one post defender in the block. He can defend an imaginary offensive post player, a manager or a coach, if you do not have a player available for that position (diagram 52).

When the guard penetrates, the post defender comes up to help (diagram 53). If penetration is stopped, the guard looks to pass to the offensive post player (diagram 54). The post defender must either stop the ball or make the ball change direction. He will try to force the guard to make an exceptional move.

When you first teach this drill, do not use a defender on the guard, i.e., do not have a defender chase the offensive guard and attempt to deflect the ball. By eliminating this position, the drill is less chaotic and easier to teach.

The post defender will now drop step, regroup, and attempt to block the post player's shot (diagram 55). The post defender must go to the outside of the offensive post player's back and attempt to block the shot with his right hand. He should use his left hand on the opposite (diagram 56).

At times we want the post defender to cheat toward the offensive post player and anticipate the pass from the guard. The guard should be able to read this and take the ball to the basket if he is not out of control. The offensive post player must create a passing lane for the guard. He must face the basket when he receives the ball so that he can quickly shoot the ball before the post defender recovers. Do this for two minutes every day.

To Take Your Game to the Next Level, Remember:
A charge is as intimidating as a blocked shot.

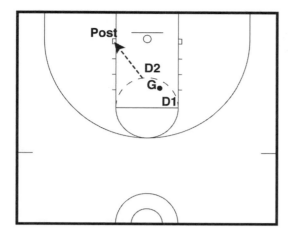

Diagram 54

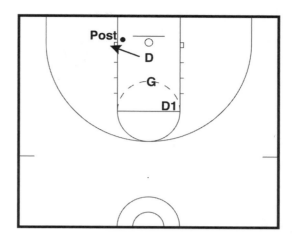

Diagram 55

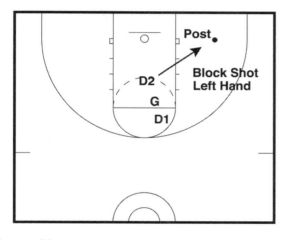

Diagram 56

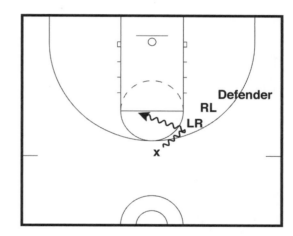

Diagram 57

Make the Ball Change Direction

When the ball is coming down the floor, most players will always dribble with their strong hand. The defender must make the ball change direction. Split the dribbler in half by overplaying the strong hand. Force the ball into the offensive player's weak hand (diagram 57). When he dribbles the ball into a shot area with his weak hand, he will have to bring the shot right back into the defense, e.g., a right-handed player will bring the ball from his left hand to his right hand to shoot a jump shot. Very few players can convert with their weak hand.

Change direction drill

Three players are needed for this drill (diagram 58). The offense is at the right elbow with the ball. Place a dummy offensive post player at the oppo-

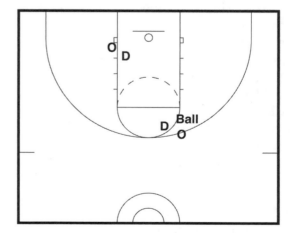

Diagram 58

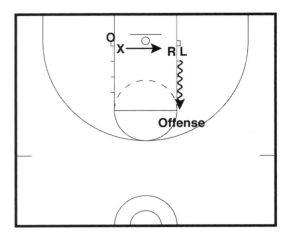

Diagram 59

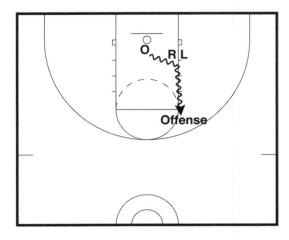

Diagram 60

Diagram 61

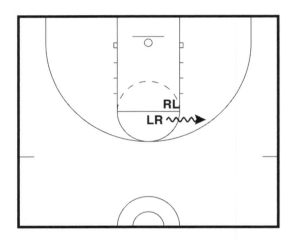

Diagram 62

site block. The post defender is at the opposite block.

The man with the ball dribbles with his right hand at the block opposite the post players. The post defender cuts off the offensive player. The post defender must straddle the line with his right foot in the paint and his left foot out. He is just above the first marker (diagram 59). The defender attempts to take the charge. If he does not take the charge, then the defender changes the direction of the dribbler. After changing the dribbler's direction, the defender recovers and attempts to block the shot with his right hand over the dribbler's outside shoulder. The offensive player changes direction and attempts to score on the left side (diagram 60). The offense gets four dribbles.The offense will work on four different moves in order to change direction.

- Day 1—Crossover
- Day 2—Through the legs
- Day 3—Reverse dribble (Remember to keep the ball in the same hand when you spin. Pull the ball through)
- Day 4—Behind your back

The offensive player must get his steps—he must jump off his inside foot. The offensive player must use a left-handed shot when starting at the right elbow (diagram 61). Rotate the drill to the left elbow. Do the drill for two minutes.

Five-second drill

If you have 12 men on your team, break into six pairs with each pair at a basket. The coach stands in the middle and controls the drill with a whistle. (Normally we will not use a whistle in practice.

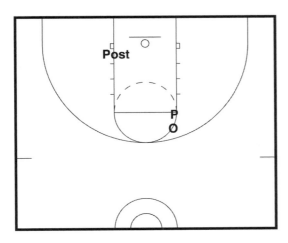

Diagram 63

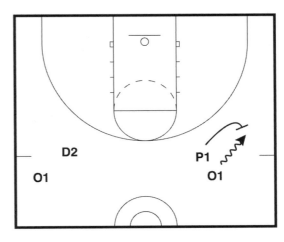

Diagram 64

Without a whistle, players become familiar with the coach's voice and commands. This drill is an exception.)

Each player works on defense for only five seconds. Each player goes on defense three times. Each pair works for 30 seconds. The team will be tired from doing 30 seconds of this drill.

The defense hands the ball to the offense at the foul line. The defense stays below the foul line. The offense stays right on the foul line. The defense touches the hip and splits the offensive player in half upon handing the ball over to him. Since the offensive player is right-handed, the defensive player will touch him with his right hand (diagram 62). In order to touch the offensive player's hip, the defensive player must bend his knees and lower his rump. In other words, the defensive player must get in stance.

The offense dribbles once to his right. He does not start the dribble until the defense touches his hip. As the offense dribbles to the right, the defensive player attempts to flick the ball with his inside hand. The offensive player will attempt to protect the ball by dribbling on his right hip. As he picks up the ball, the offensive player jump stops and pivots on his right foot. The offensive player looks to pass to the post (diagram 63).

As the offensive player picks up the ball to pass to the post, the defensive player comes up to the offensive player. The defensive player goes belly to belly with the offensive player as he brings the ball up. The defender is within three feet of the offensive player. As the offensive player brings the ball over his head, the defensive player brings his hands over his head to mirror the ball. The defender crosses his forearms with his palms facing the offensive player. We call this position "crossface." By crossing his forearms, the defensive player takes away the passing lane into the post from the offensive player.

Continue the drill to the left side. The offense will now attempt to dribble once to his left. The defender must split the offensive player with his left hand on the offensive player's hip.

By using the crossface technique, we can deny the entry pass into the post and thus help our post defenders. The player attempting to make the post entry cannot see the offensive post player if his defender is using the crossface technique.

The defender on the ball causes the ballhandler to pick up his dribble. The defender uses the crossface technique to block the passing lanes. The defender off the ball completely denies the pass (diagram 64).

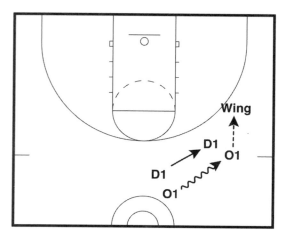
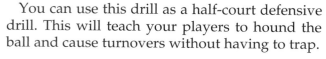

Diagram 65

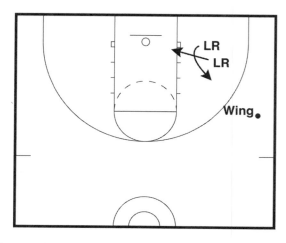

Diagram 66

You can use this drill as a half-court defensive drill. This will teach your players to hound the ball and cause turnovers without having to trap.

Combination drill

The ball handler dribbles to the right side. The defense tries to split him while flicking at the ball. When the ball handler picks up his dribble, the defender will use the crossface technique. The ball handler will attempt to pass to the wing at the foul line extended. The defender will jump into the passing lane and deny the return pass (diagram 65).

The defender will jump to the ball and will force the cutter behind him. The defender will find the cutter, and the cutter will dive into the ball-side block. The defender will deny the side high. The wing will attempt an entry pass to the post. If the post scores, start the drill from the beginning with a dribble at the wing. The defender remains as defense. If the post entry is not made, the cutter goes to the ball side, i.e., right corner.

The defender must deny the ball into the corner. The defender must keep inside the forearm on the cutter in order to continue contact. The defender, however, must be careful not to overplay. He must use his right hand and not his body to deny. The cutter goes backdoor if the defender overplays him. The cutter then will drop his left foot and seal the defender for the backdoor cut. He must use his left forearm to create the seal (diagram 66).

If the cutter catches the ball in ball side, i.e., right corner, he will reverse pivot. The offense has two dribbles in order to score. The defender will get within three feet of the offensive player with his hand on the offensive player's left hip. The defender will split the offensive player. The defender will force the offensive player to the midpoint baseline area behind the backboard.

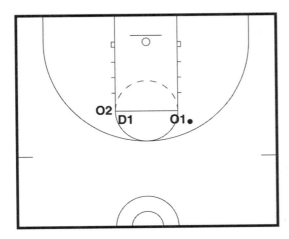

Diagram 67

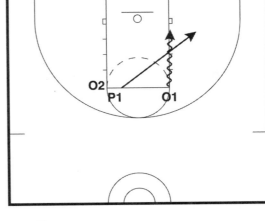

Diagram 68

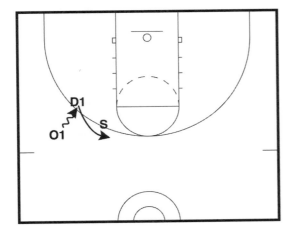

Diagram 69

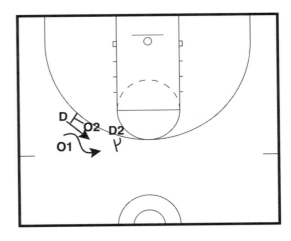

Diagram 70

Block the shot drill

This drill teaches the defense how to block shots. It is important to note that the possibility of a blocked shot intimidates an offensive player. Offense is learning how to finish the break. The baby hook shot is also learned.

If you have 12 men on your team, break into four groups of three players each. The offensive player with the ball will line up at the right elbow. The defender will line up at the opposite elbow defending another offensive player one-pass-away. He denies the pass (diagram 67). The offensive player with the ball will dribble hard at the right block. He will attempt to score shooting a baby hook shot. The defender will open up and chase the ball attempting to block the shot (diagram 68). The defender will go to the shooter's outside shoulder. The defender will use his inside,

i.e., left hand to block the shot. If the defender misses the block, he runs by the shooter. This way the defender avoids fouling the shooter.

Rotate to the left side and continue the drill. Now the offensive player with the ball has an opportunity to work his left hand.

Screen-and-roll

How many ways can you play screen-and-roll?

It is important to never let a screen-and-roll team go the same way every time. The defender on the ball can follow the man over the top. The defender on the ball must force the ball over the screen and away from the baseline. The defender must force the ball handler to make a V movement (diagram 69).

The defender on the screener must get up and hedge (diagram 70). The defender on the screen

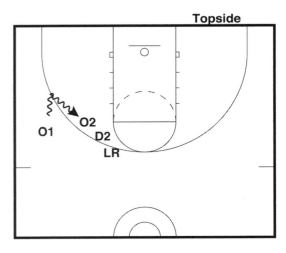

Diagram 71

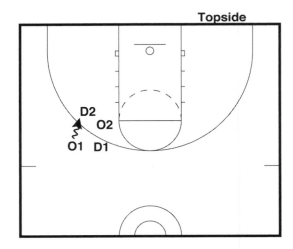

Diagram 72

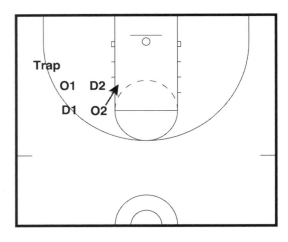

Diagram 73

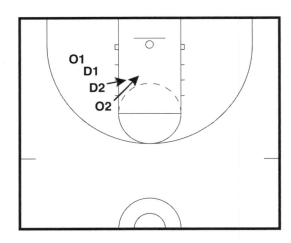

Diagram 74

must keep one hand on the screener and show his other hand at the dribbler. In this case, his right hand is on the screener and his left hand is being shown at the ball handler. The defender on the screener will front him when he rolls. By keeping a hand on the screener, the defender will know when he rolls and will stay with him.

The defender on the ball can go under the screen. He can go under the screen when the ball handler is outside his range. Force the ball handler to make a V movement. The defender on the screener plays topside and hedge (diagram 71). The defender must keep one hand on the screener. The defender on the ball goes under the screen. The defender on the ball can play topside, and the defender on the screen can play baseline side (diagram 72).

Do not allow the ball to the middle. Chase the ball to the midpoint baseline area. Trap with both defenders toward the baseline. (diagram 73) Rotate with the defender of the screen fronting his man (diagram 74). Both defenders can trap.

One day, work on forcing the ball over the top. The next day, work on going under the screen. The next, work on playing topside. Finally, work on trapping.

Post screen drill

This is a two-minute drill. When defending a screener, open topside to ball-you-man (diagram 75). Do not let the offensive player post up after he sets the screen. Always take away one of the sides from the receiver of the screen (diagram 76). If you take away the backdoor, he will curl.

Follow the cutter if he has good shooting range (diagram 77). The screener's defender must help here. Shoot the gap if he has no shooting range

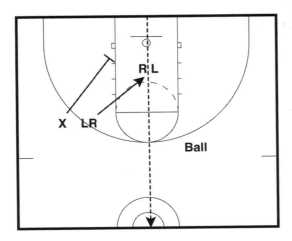

Diagram 75

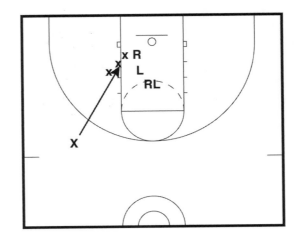

Diagram 76

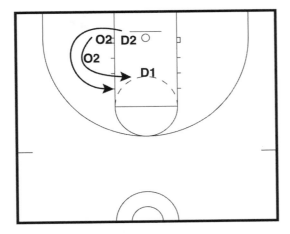

Diagram 77

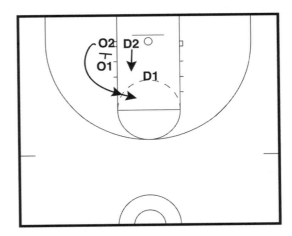

Diagram 78

(diagram 78). Let him fade. Bump and take away the curl completely. Close out if he fades (diagram 79). On the first day we will work on following the cutter. On the second day we will work on shooting the gap. On the final day, we will work on bumping.

We want our guys to understand that when a screener goes down to screen, the screener's defender never turns his head and does not close up. Why? Our reason is that the bottom defender can't get through. Anytime your man goes to screen, you always open up, play on the top side, and let the defender underneath decide whether he is going to curl with the curler or shoot the gap.

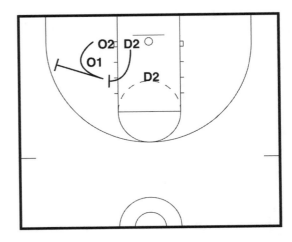

Diagram 79

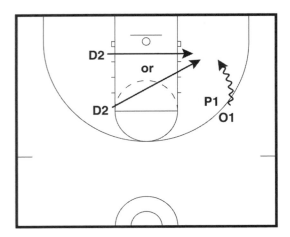

Diagram 80

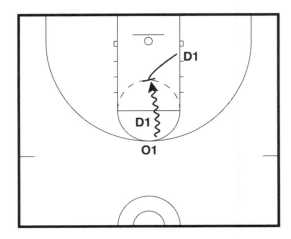

Diagram 81

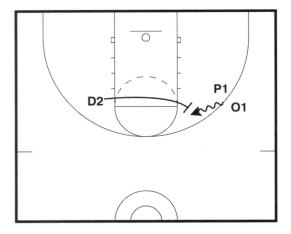

Diagram 82

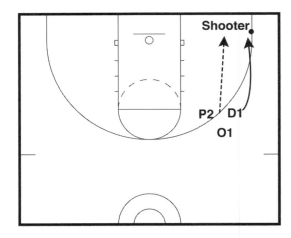

Diagram 83

Where do you want to trap?

Trap areas when a teammate is beaten. Set the trap outside the lane block area from the post or high when your teammate is beaten from the wing (diagram 80). The offensive player cannot elevate outside the lane area. Take charge or set the trap with the beaten defender.

Set the trap on the dotted line or the first marker (diagram 81). Rotate and trap outside the foul line area when a teammate is beaten at the wing and the offensive player drives to the middle. Keep

the offensive player outside the foul-line area. We want the offensive player shooting no closer than three feet from the foul line (diagram 82). When you trap down from high, always run at the outside shoulder of the shooter. He will not be able to see you coming at him (diagram 83).

Trap and react drill

When the point guard is able to beat his man, the nearest wing defender comes to help. The back defender plays two offensive players (diagram 84).

To Take Your Game to the Next Level: If the man defending you leaves you to trap elsewhere, you are responsible to create a passing lane for the offensive player being trapped.

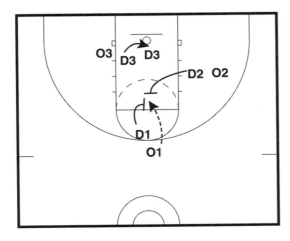

Diagram 84

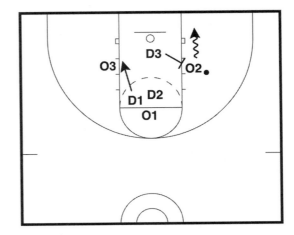

Diagram 85

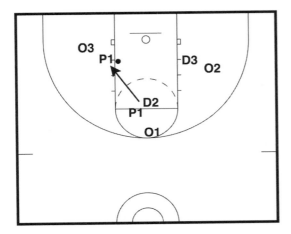

Diagram 86

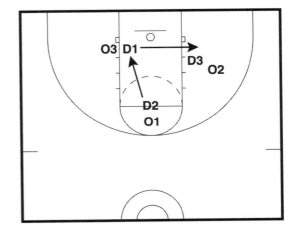

Diagram 87

The defender coming to the trap is responsible for sealing the trap. He must not let the offensive player split the trap.

The back man, D3, takes O2 on the first pass (diagram 85). He takes away the middle from O2. D2 stays with O1. The defender who is beaten, in this case D1, rotates down and takes D3's man, O3. We will not ask a player to run and trap and then run and trap again, so D2 stays with O1 (diagram 86). D1 will come over with D3 and trap O2 on the baseline if D3 is beaten. D2 must drop and cover O3 (diagram 87). If the pass goes from O2 back to O1, D1 stays with O2, D2 rotates to O1, and D3 moves over to O3 (diagram 88).

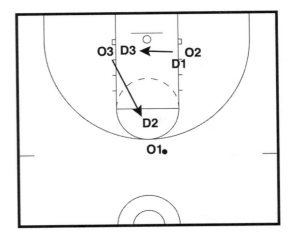

Diagram 88

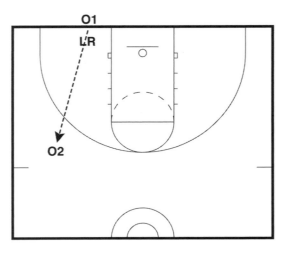

Diagram 89

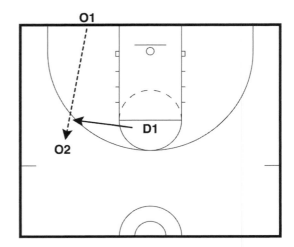

Diagram 90

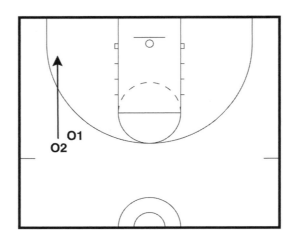

Diagram 91

If the offense shoots and scores, they keep the ball. Offense becomes defense when the offense shoots and the defense gets the ball. Work on this drill for two minutes each day.

In this drill, we are practicing beating the trap with a pass, splitting the trap, creating passing lanes, and scoring. Defensively, we are working on trapping, defending the split, denying the shot, and defensive rotation.

Out-of-bounds drill

There are many teams today that run sideline break after a basket. How do you defend against this? We designate a player to defend the inbounds pass. He will overplay his "man 1/2 man" to his left. He will jump and be athletic using the crossface technique. He will attempt to deny the passing lane to the outlet man (diagram 89). Since most players are right-handed, they will throw this pass from the right side of the offensive court. As the coach, you will have to make the appropriate adjustments if the pass is made on the other side.

Our guard must quickly find the outlet man. He must get on the same plane between the passer and the outlet man (diagram 90). Then the defender must run at the outlet man. He then denies the pass, forcing the outlet man below the foul line (diagram 91). Once the ball is inbounded, the defender on the ball must turn the ball handler twice before they reach half court. By this time all four other defenders are back.

Timing of drills

Use three baskets, with four men at a basket. Drill just as described above. Start with two offensive players. When they score, they become defense. They must stop the other two players from running a sideline break. Go for two minutes.

This is the toughest thing to teach your team besides offensive rebounding. After a score your team is accustomed to getting back to the paint in defensive transition. You want to teach your team not to let your opponents run their fast break offense after you score.

You can do all these drills every day. It will take you about 20 minutes to complete them. Certainly, these drills will make your team better defensively.

Drill	Time
One-on-One	2 minutes
Steals and Deflections	2 minutes
Change of Direction	2 minutes
Five-Second Drill	Alternate for 30 seconds
Combo	2 minutes
Block the Shot	2 minutes
Screen-and-Roll	2 minutes
Post Screen	2 minutes
Trap and React	2 minutes

Defensive Drill Mania

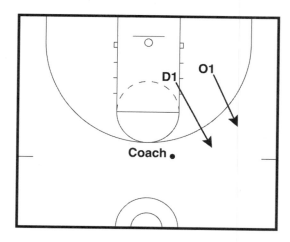

Diagram 92

Out-of-Bounds   2 minutes

Top Ten List of Defensive Rules and Concepts

1. Ball-you-man
2. On line, up line
3. Inside foot and inside hand up on the wing
   - Head in chest numbers.
   - Hands active. Dig hand and up hand.
4. Force the offensive man toward one direction
   - Toward the baseline.
   - Don't get beat in the middle.
5. Shoulders are parallel to the sideline
6. Meet the post flashing high and force high
7. Jump to the pass
8. Do not let the cutter get in front of you
9. When in transition defense, get back to the paint and pan out to the offense—stop the ball first
10. Communicate

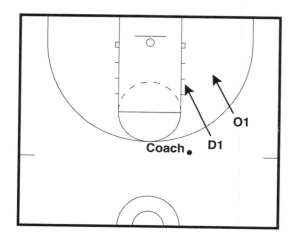

Diagram 93

Denial Drills

One-on-one denial

Start with the coach having the ball. O1 cuts to the wing. D1 denies him (diagram 92). O1 will then cut backdoor, and D1 will turn his head to see both the cutter and the ball. D1 must not open up!

After two or three cuts, the offense will get the pass and play one-on-one (diagram 93).

Two-on-two denial

Player O1 breaks out to the wing. D1 denies his cut. D2 jumps to help-side defense (diagram 94) and D2 has to watch out for O2 flashing into the lane (diagram 95). The coach then reverses the ball

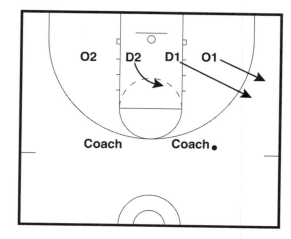

Diagram 94

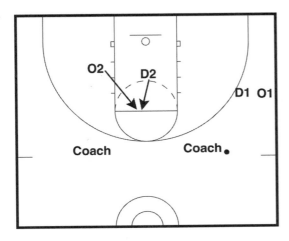

Diagram 95

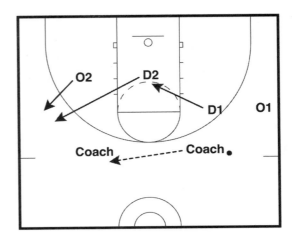

Diagram 96

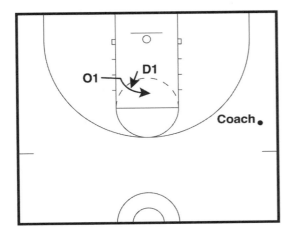

Diagram 97

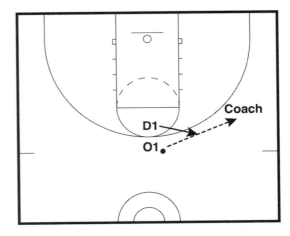

Diagram 98

to another coach. O2 cuts to the wing. D2 recovers and denies 02. D1 jumps to help-side defense (diagram 96).

One-on-one deny the flash

The coach has the ball. O1 will flash to the ball-side block. D1 will meet O1 in the middle of the lane and bump him, forcing O1 to the high post. When the offense catches the ball, they play one-on-one (diagram 97).

One-on-one basket cut

O1 has the ball and passes to the coach. D1 jumps to the pass (diagram 98). O1 makes a basket cut. D1 denies O1 the ball and does not let O1 get in front of him. When O1 gets to the block, D1 fronts the post (diagram 99).

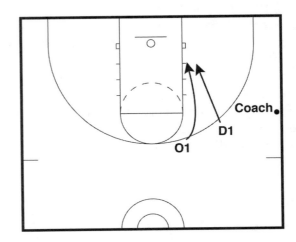

Diagram 99

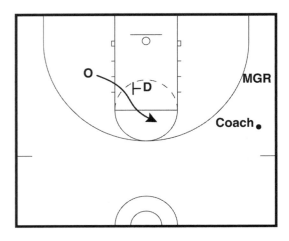

Diagram 100

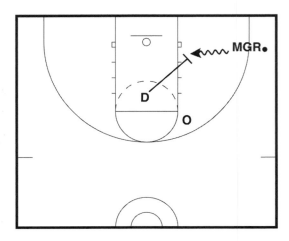

Diagram 101

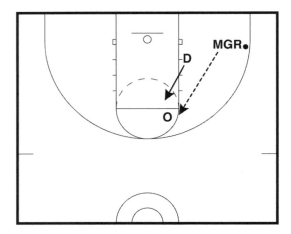

Diagram 102

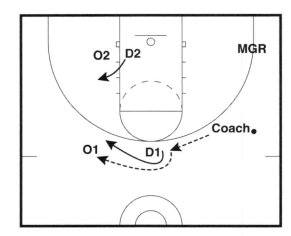

Diagram 103

Help Drills

Deny flash post and help baseline

Player O flashes to the ball side. D denies O by meeting and bumping him in the lane. The coach throws the ball to the manager (diagram 100). The manager drives the baseline. D comes over to stop the drive and meets the ball outside the lane (diagram 101). When the ball is stopped, the manager then throws to O. D recovers to O and they play one-on-one (diagram 102).

Two-on-two guard rotation with help on baseline

The coach drives the ball to the middle and then passes to O1. D1 helps and recovers to O1. D2 shifts over to guard O2 (diagram 103). O2 breaks out to the wing. D2 will deny (diagram 104). You

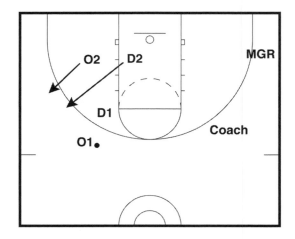

Diagram 104

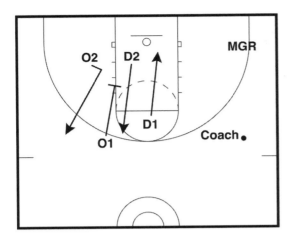

Diagram 105

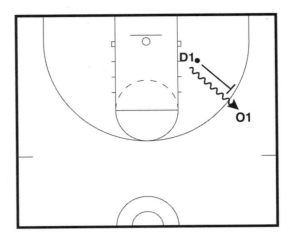

Diagram 106

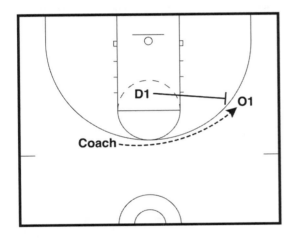

Diagram 107

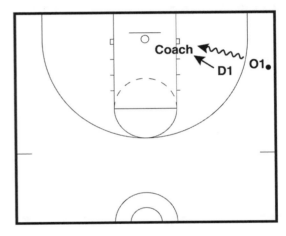

Diagram 108

may start the drill with O2 screening for O1 (diagram 105). D1 must let D2 slip though the screen.

Close-Out Series

One-on-one close out

D1 passes to O1. D1 closes out on O1 and they play one-on-one (diagram 106). Coach has the ball on the opposite wing. D1 is in help position. Coach passes to O1. D1 closes out on O1 and they play one-on-one (diagram 107).

One-on-one root down

O1 passes to coach in the post. D1 will root down on the post but will stay open to O1 (diagram 108). It is important that D1 only roots down when the coach bounces the ball.

Coach will pass out to O1. D1 will recover to O1 and they play one-on-one (diagram 109).

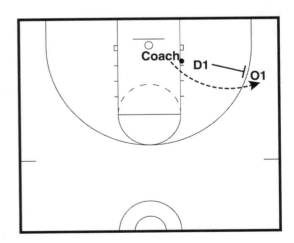

Diagram 109

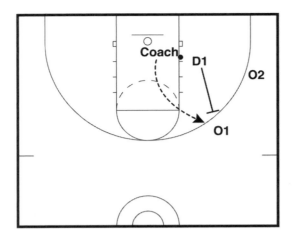

Diagram 110

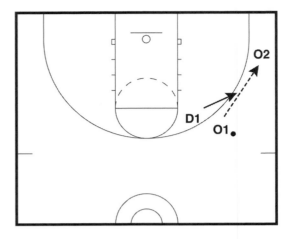

Diagram 111

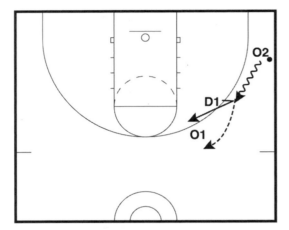

Diagram 112

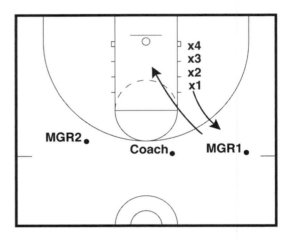

Diagram 113

Two-on-one close out

The coach passes to O1, D1 closes out on O1 (diagram 110). O1 passes to O2. D1 jumps to the pass (diagram 111). O2 drives to the middle. D1 helps. O2 then passes to O1. D1 recovers and they play one-on-one (diagram 112).

Team Defense

Team denial drill

X1 slides up to the wing yelling "deny" to the manager. Then he contests the manager's shot. X1 slides back down to the block, turning his head to see the ball, which is now in the coach's hands at the top of the key (diagram 113).

X1 slides across the lane yelling "help" until he gets to the opposite block. Then he slides up to the wing and contests the second manager's

shot. At the same time, X2 starts his denial on the opposite wing (diagram 114).

X1 will deny back down to the block watching the coach with the ball at the top of the key. X2 continues to slide across the lane and then up to the manager (MGR2). X3 starts his drill at the same time (diagram 115). At any time, the coach may throw the ball to a defender who does not see him.

Four-on-four shell (diagram 116) and four-on-three shell (diagram 117)

The drill starts when the coach throws the ball to either O1 or O2. D1 will guard the ball. Then it is a scramble. One defender will be guarding two people and must call that out. On the pass, the defense must jump to the ball. Each defender must

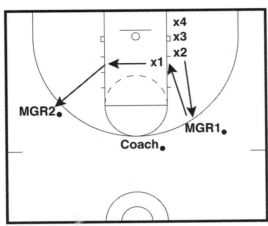

Diagram 114

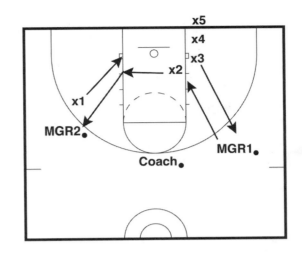

Diagram 115

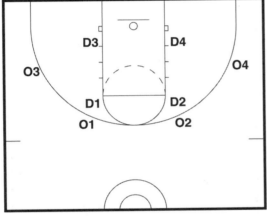

Diagram 116

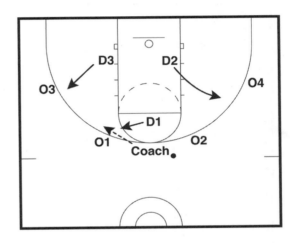

Diagram 117

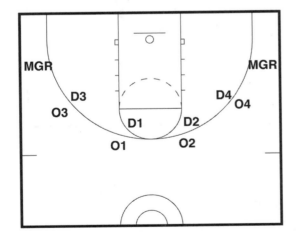

Diagram 118

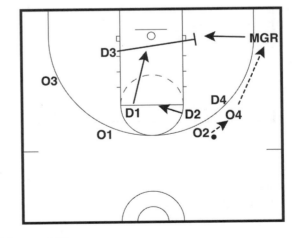

Diagram 119

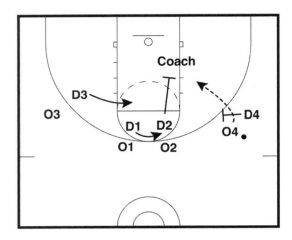

Diagram 120

Diagram 121

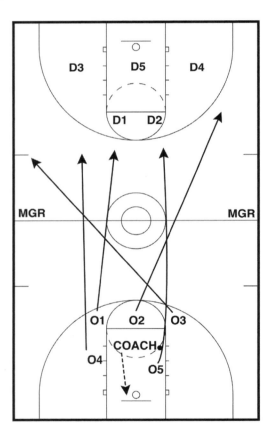

Diagram 122

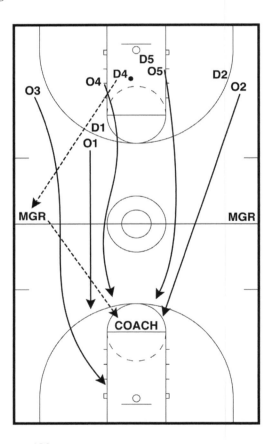

Diagram 123

call out "ball," "help" and "I got two." The defender closest to the ball covers it.

Six-on-four shell

Set up as shown in diagram 118 with a manager in each corner. When the ball is passed to the manager, the manager drives to the basket. D3 will stop the drive. D1 will rotate down. D2 will guard both O1 and O2 up top. D4 stays with O4. (diagram 119).

Four-on-four with open posts

We will work on our "squeezing" out of this drill. For example, if O4 passes to the coach in the post, we may say that D2 will double-down on the post. The ball-side defender never leaves his

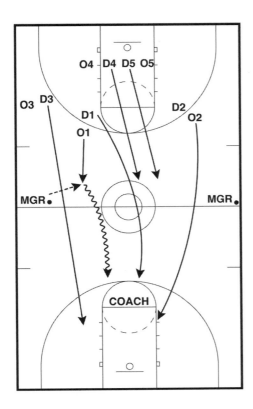

Diagram 124

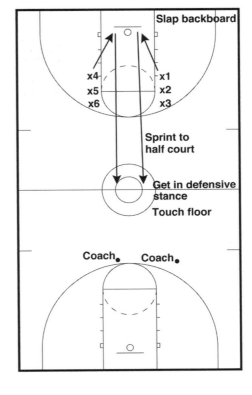

Diagram 125

man, D4. D1 will rotate to O2. D3 yells "I got two" and guards O3 and O1 (diagram 120). When the ball is passed out, the squeeze man (D2) goes opposite the pass, e.g., coach throws the ball to O2. D3 guards O1, D2 will go out opposite and guard O3 (diagram 121).

Transition drills from offense to defense

The coach throws the ball up at the glass. The offense rebounds and attacks the defense (diagram 122). The defense can be in any position they want. The offense has to make their adjustments.

After the shot is taken and the defense gets the rebound on a make or miss, the defense outlets to the manager. The manager passes the ball to the coach. The new defensive team must get back and deflect the pass to the coach (diagram 123). After a shot is taken, the coach designates a guard to run to the manager and gets the outlet pass. The guard then drives the ball to the basket and the defense has to stop his penetration (diagram 124).

Full-court defensive drill

Players line up on elbows facing basket. X4 and X1 jump and slap the backboard. They turn and sprint to half court. At half court they get in a de-

fensive stance as if they were defending a ball handler (diagram 125). X4 and X1 will slide to the sidelines. X5 and X2 jump and slap the backboard. They turn and spring to half court. When X4 and X1 reach the sideline, they get in their stance as if they were denying the passing lane. When they reach the baseline, X4 and X1 get in line behind the coaches to continue the rotation (diagram 126).

O1 and D1 play one-on-one. X's are coaches, managers or other players. The X's should be lined up straight down the court on the same line as the lane line. If the ball goes outside the lane line extended, it is a turnover (diagram 127). The coach throws the ball to any of the offensive players (in this case, O3). D3, who is guarding O3, runs and touches the baseline (diagram 128). O3 outlets the ball to O1 and the offense breaks. D1 and D2 have to get back to the paint area and stop the ball. D3 trails and gets back defensively (diagram 129).

Half-court fire drill

Four offensive players stand on the three-point line. The offensive players can only pass the ball around with no dribbling. Three defensive players have 30 seconds to rotate and scramble to guard the ball. Defenders not on the ball are in a

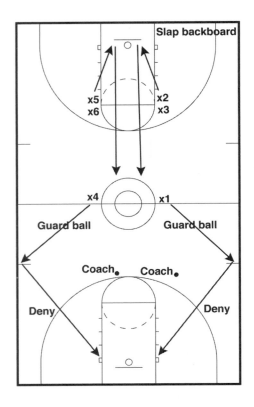

Diagram 126

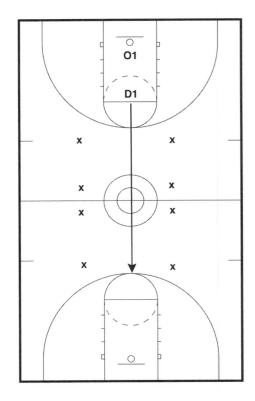

Diagram 127

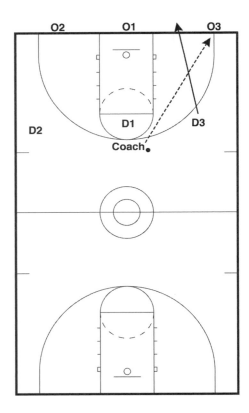

Diagram 128

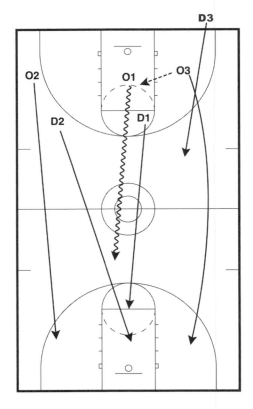

Diagram 129

position to help in the weak side. The defender closest to the ball will guard it. The other two defenders must be ready to take the next pass and rotate. This drill will teach close outs, communication, rotation and weak-side help.

Full-court fire drill

This is a five-on-five full-court drill. When the coach blows the whistle, the player with the ball will simply drop it where he is. He and his teammates will become the defense. However, they are not allowed to cover the same man that was covering them. This will force a scrambling situation, where all the players will not be able to guard the same person who was guarding them.

Coaches can make this drill into a game, where teams get points for baskets, steals, deflections, charges, rebounds, successful transitions into defense, etc. This drill teaches communication, rotation and transition defense.

Full-court shell drill

Put a line in each corner of the court. The first player in each line comes out and plays defense. The next player plays offense. This gives you a four-on-four look. Standing in the middle of the court, the coach will throw the ball to any offensive player. As soon as the coach enters the ball, the drill begins. The coach will assign the baskets for each team.

Defenders will learn midline help, forcing the ball sideline, rotation and communication. The coach can add trapping or any adjustment he wants.

Steven Culp
Akron North High School, OH

Scramble Drills

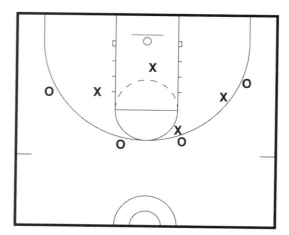

Diagram 130

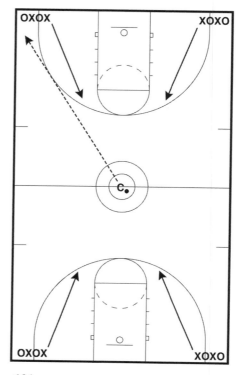

Diagram 131

This is a full-court drill with no out of bounds. The drill should be played to 16 points. Emphasis can be placed on either offensive or defensive rebounding. Three teams compete continuously during this drill. Scoring is as follows:

• Two points for offensive rebound

• One point for defensive rebound

• One point for score

The drill begins with four white jerseys trying to rebound against four blue jerseys in the half court. One team is designated the defense, while the other team is designated the offense. The coach has the basketball. He will dribble the basketball and force both teams to move. The coach will then shoot the ball. (diagram 130)

If the defensive team rebounds, they get one point. The defense will quickly outlet the ball to an assistant coach standing at the elbow at the other end of the court. The defensive team (blue jerseys) now becomes the offense and sprints down to the other end of the floor where the ball is. The four red jerseys are here waiting to play defense. They will match up to the offense. The previous offensive team (white jerseys) stays in their positions and waits to play defense (diagram 131).

If the offensive team rebounds the ball, they get two points. They will also try to score off the offensive rebound. If they score, they get another point and keep possession of the ball. They then outlet the ball to the assistant coach at the other end of the court. The offense must take the ball out of bounds before they outlet after they score in this drill. This will simulate offensive transition after a basket.

The offense will outlet the ball to the assistant coach at the other end of the floor if they do not score after their put-back attempt but still get another offensive rebound.

Variation: The offensive team will try to score off every offensive rebound they get, so they can accumulate multiple rebound points. Once the offense scores, they will take the ball out of bounds, inbound it to the assistant coach, and push the ball up the floor where the defense is waiting. If your team outlets the ball, you are still on offense.

Dagan Nelson
SUNY New Paltz, NY

Four-on-Four Rebounding in the Full Court

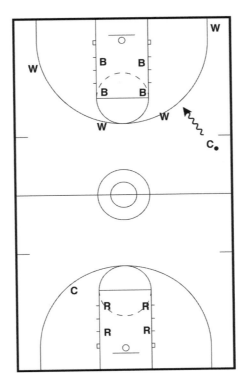

Diagram 132

The game is played to 16. Each coach takes a team and keeps their score (diagram 132).

Points of emphasis:

- Hit and hold your block-out.
- Pursue the ball when it is not in your area.
- Develop an attacking mentality. Do not give in to being blocked out. This drill can create the mentality you want in your players for attacking the glass.

W=white

B=blue

R=rebounder

C=coach

O=basketball

Stance and Box-Out Drill

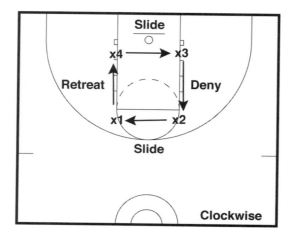

Diagram 133

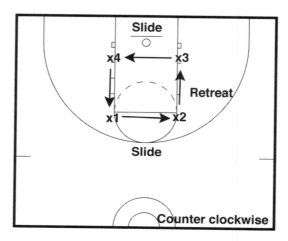

Diagram 134

This drill works on footwork, conditioning, finding your box-out responsibility, and using the different types of box-outs. This is a great drill for teaching boxing out from any zone defense.

Players line up with two players at the elbows and two players on the blocks. Players will move in a clockwise or counterclockwise position, depending upon the coach's command. Players will work on their slide step, retreat step, or post denial step, depending on which direction they are going (diagram 133 and 134).

Upon the command of "box," players will locate and box out an imaginary offensive player. The rotation is similar to the above drills. Players sprint to the opposite baseline or half court upon command of "break." Offensive players can "dummy-up" and remain motionless in order to teach defenders how to locate offensive rebounders. The drill can also go live (diagram 135).

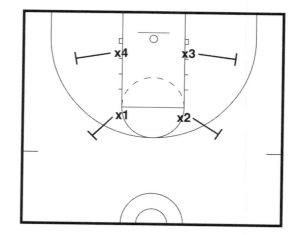

Diagram 135

Kevin Pigott
Fordham Preparatory School, NY

Rebounding – The Tough Drill

This is a defensive rebounding drill which incorporates some shell fundamentals. It reinforces the importance of ball awareness and blocking out. You'll need a half court, one ball and nine players.

Start with three offensive players around the perimeter and three defenders on them. The offensive players pass the ball around while the defensive team works on ball-you-man positioning (shell drill). The coach gives a signal (whistle or verbal), and whoever has the ball takes the shot. Everything counts as a miss, so if the shooter hits the shot, they must rebound it out of the net.

All defensive players and players on the baseline must yell "shot" and then "box" when the shot goes up to give the defenders an audio cue to block out. We make them do pushups if they don't make these calls. The team also does not score a point for a defensive rebound if they do not communicate.

Players on defense attempt to block out the offensive team. Whichever team gets the rebound stays on, and the other team rotates off. If the defense gets the rebound, they are given a point. A new group comes in on offense, and the drill starts again.

Also, we set up this drill to cover things our next opponent will do to us. For example, we will begin the drill with a pick-and-roll by the offensive team, or we may begin with a double-screen-down for a shooter. Be creative!

A few things to think about...
You can only score a point if you are on defense to start the drill. So essentially, a team must first get an offensive board before they can get on defense and begin to score points. Play to five, and don't call a lot of fouls here.

Adam Parmenter
Five-Star Basketball Camp
Mercy College, NY

Shell Defense Series

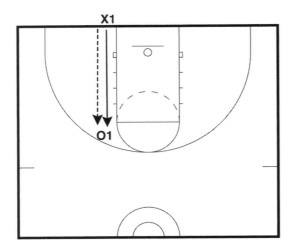

Diagram 136

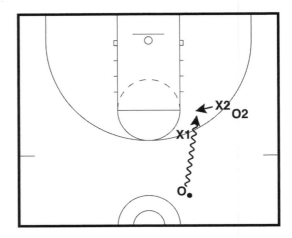

Diagram 137

The following series of drills can be used individually or in tandem to build up to a full five-on-five team defensive system. Take your individual principles, concepts and terminology and apply them throughout the series of drills. Just like no offense is perfectly suited to your players without some manipulation, no defense is perfectly suited without some changes.

One-on-One —On the Ball Defense

Roll-out/close-out drill

X1 rolls ball to O1 at elbow, closes out and touches O1 on the hip, O1 goes live (Diagram 136). Limit the number of dribbles to two or three per possession. This requires O1 to make a solid, game-condition move and X1 to work harder to try to stop it. You can change the start position of O1 to the top of the key, wing, either block, etc. Tailor the drill to the spots where players will catch in your offense, or the offense of upcoming opponent.

Two-on-Two—Shell Help and Recover

Help and recover drill

O1 has the ball at the top of the key, X1 allows O1 to beat him off the dribble to the outside. X2 must step slide to cut off O1's penetration (Diagram 137). O1 either dishes to O2, in which case X2 must close out hard at O2 and force to the baseline midpoint, or retreat dribbles to the top of the key, in which case X2 must close out to deny O2 (Diagram 138).

Jump to the ball, jump to the passing lane

The ball starts with O1 at the top of the key, with an offensive teammate on the wing (diagram 139). The defensive player on ball (X1) yells "ball," the defender on the wing denies (or helps, depending on your philosophy) and must make verbal cue "deny" or "help."

O1 passes to O2 on the wing. X1 "jumps" to the passing lane; meaning the first step is backward, the second slide is into the passing lane. This defends initially against a possible give-and-go cut

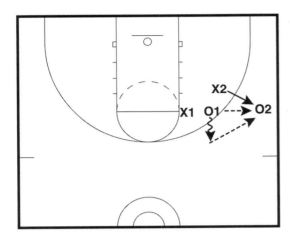

Diagram 138

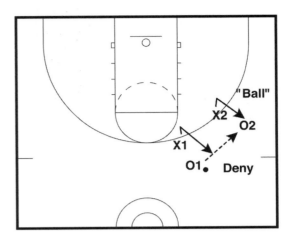

Diagram 139

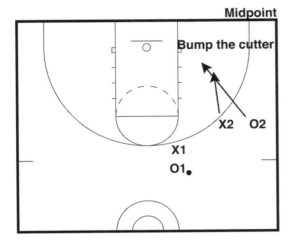

Diagram 140

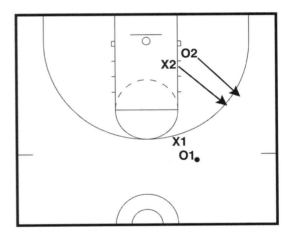

Diagram 141

by O1 and denies a reversal. X2 "jumps" to the ball. The first step is backward, the second slide is into an on-the-ball defensive position. The inside foot is high, forcing offensive player to the midpoint on the baseline.

Guarding the cutter

O1 has the ball at the top of the key. O2 is being denied by X2 and makes cut from wing to block. X2 must slide (foot-foot-midpoint), bumping O2's cut and forcing the cutter toward the midpoint (diagram 140). O2 must cut hard, plant at block/midpoint and cut hard back to the wing. X2 continues to deny as O2 cuts back out to the wing (diagram 141). X1 must trace the ball with his hands, focusing on forcing a bad pass or tipping pass while defending against possible dribble penetration.

NOTE: These three fundamental aspects of wing/guard play can be shuffled as well as played live. Tell the offense to focus on drive and kick or whichever aspect you feel an upcoming opponent features or that your players are having trouble defending. Also, this is the perfect time to mix in your screen-and-roll defenses in the two-man game setting.

Three-on-Three —Shell Help and Recover

Shell defense with concern for the post

Introduce post defense and your approach with this drill. By adding a third player in the post, all of the two-on-two shell drills above can be run, adding a downscreen or backscreen on the pass to the wing, as well as post defense.

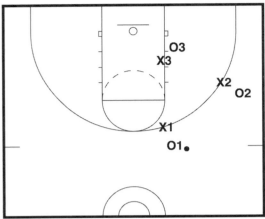

Diagram 142

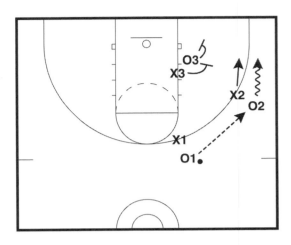

Diagram 143

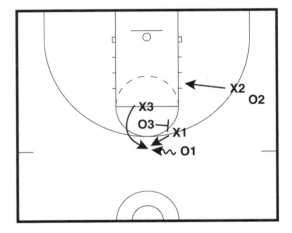

Diagram 144

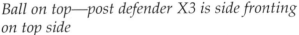

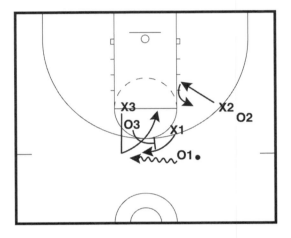

Diagram 145

Ball on top—post defender X3 is side fronting on top side

Ball is passed to the wing (diagram 142). The post defender either fronts or kick punches to the bottom side, depending on the level of the offensive player and your philosophy. The general concept is to have a post player front the pass from the wing, which is a tough angle for a lob pass, especially with weak side help available, and kick punch under when the ball is toward the baseline (diagram 143). Some teams may find it necessary to dead front the post anytime the ball is under the foul line extended on the wing.

Use the post as a screener, with the third defensive player helping according to your coverage scheme. If you normally blitz or trap the ballhandler, the third defender must jump to help cover the roll man and spy his man on a kickout (diagram 144). If you hedge and recover, a third defender should be available if the screener slips quickly to the basket (diagram 145). Adjust this portion of the drill to your defensive preferences.

Wing-wing-point shell defense

This shell formation introduces the concept of two-passes-away (diagram 146). If the ball is passed from point to wing, X3 slides to help position, since O3 is now two passes away from the ball (diagram 147). X2 must jump to the ball, and X1 must jump to the passing lane to deny. If the ball is passed back to point, X3 recovers to deny, since O3 is now one pass away. You must choose your preference for both one-pass and two-passes away. Will you deny the wing, or drop to help when one-pass-away? And if two-passes-away,

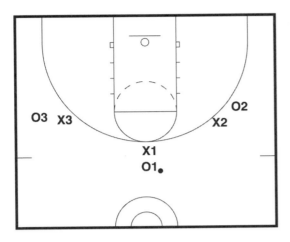

Diagram 146

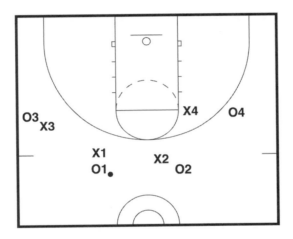

Diagram 147

Diagram 148

will you help and exactly how much? Put this philosophy into play in this drill.

You can mix in simple offensive movements such as passing and screening away, passing and cutting through and replacing, and others. Players must know when to drop to help as the player they guard moves from one-pass to two-passes away. Also, they must learn proper ball-you-man principles by keeping an eye on the ball and adjusting their position for its movement.

Four-on-Four—Perimeter Team Shell

Classic two-guard two-wing shell drill

This is a classic shell format, with basic perimeter positions for many offensive sets including flex, some four-out-one in motion, and two-three high sets (diagram 148). Players must communicate whether they are one-pass or two-passes

away. Be sure to have them say "one-pass," "two passes," "deny," "help" or "ball" to let teammates know which position they are in. Diagram 148 shows the initial setup and the initial position of defenders who are denying one-pass away, and helping two-passes away.

Initially, have offensive players pass and hold for a three- to five-second count in order to check defensive positioning and footwork. Then speed up the drill. Focus on having players move during the flight of the ball, not after it is caught.

Try this for an advanced drill: As the ball moves from side to side, have the opposite offensive players exchange positions and later screen away so that the defensive players must move to correct positions while guarding general offensive strategies.

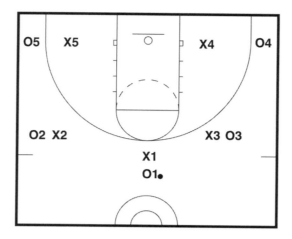

Diagram 149

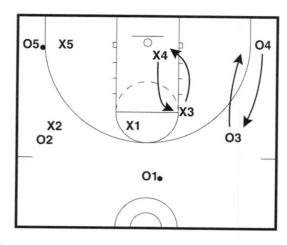

Diagram 150

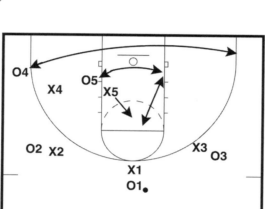

Diagram 151

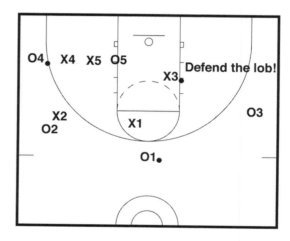

Diagram 152

Five-on-Five—Team Shell: Tying It All Together

Perimeter Shell: point-wing-wing-corner-corner

This is another classic perimeter-oriented shell that focuses completely on perimeter defense (diagram 149). The baseline defenders drop to the help position immediately as their offensive players are two-passes away. Wing defenders are in deny position as they are one-pass away. This shell mimics a five-out motion offense and gets your perimeter defenders involved in defending and positioning themselves based on any combination of ball-and-man position on the perimeter.

Diagram 150 shows defensive positioning as the ball is in a corner, as well as defensive movement to coordinate with offensive movement exchanging on the opposite side of the floor. You can get

as creative as you want with this drill. Have players cut through and replace, exchange, and have offensive players simulate dribble drive situations where defenders must help and recover. Tailor this drill to your game plan and come back to it to simulate tendencies of your upcoming opponents.

Four-man shell with a post

For this drill, initially the post player sets up on one block and remains stationary. Later on, the post can move block to block and even to the high post while the corner offensive player can run the baseline corner to corner (diagram 151). Defensive alignments now have to take into account defending the pass into the post. If you are fronting, there always should be protection from the lob pass, even in an overload situation such as that which is created by our initial setup (diagram 152).

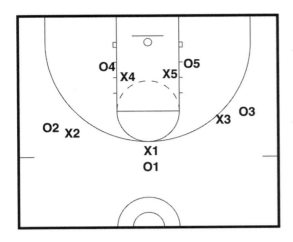

Diagram 153

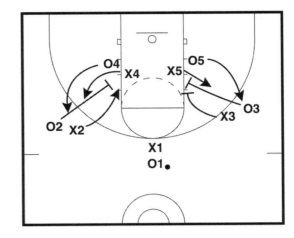

Diagram 154

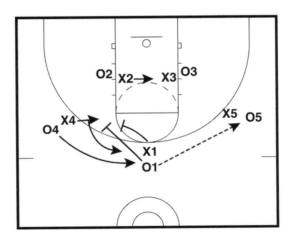

Diagram 155

Three-out-two-in shell drill

This drill introduces concepts in defending offenses with double posts. Initially you will line up with an offensive player on each block, two wings and a point (diagram 153). In addition to covering ball movement, which will follow exactly as covered in the previous drills, this drill introduces team concepts and off-the-ball screens. Classic motion concepts of screening down (diagram 154) and passing then screening away (diagram 155) should be mixed in.

This makes every defensive player learn every spot on the court and every screen coverage. Initially, have defenders fight over every screen by getting between the cutter and screener or by locking on to the cutter's hip and sprinting to beat them out of the screen area before they can catch.

Try this for an advanced drill: Ball-side screens should be fought through and denied. Weak side screens should be easier to defend as both defenders will be in help positions.

Part Four:
Zone Defense

David Walsh
Arlington High School, NJ

Ideas About Zones

Why Zone? The Zone Misconception

By employing a zone you can limit the number of different offensive situations that you and your players will see during a game. There are only so many different ways to beat a zone. Some coaches have the idea that zone is a way to protect your players from fouling. Watch my team and you will understand how aggressive a zone defense can be. We usually have more fouls than our opponent, and these tend to be aggressive ball-hawking fouls. For a zone to work, the players must be as active as if they were playing a man defense. Man and zone defenses share many characteristics. However, it is important to remember that teaching and playing zone defense has its own particular nuances that must be followed for its success. The difference with playing a zone defense is that you can target players to play specific areas of the zone. Teaching these different rules for each position to all your players enables them to be able to play anywhere in the zone with some expectation of success because they know where to go.

What Zone Do You Choose?

Choosing a zone to play is like choosing an offense to run—it must be based on the capabilities of your players. For instance, I run a 1-2-2 because I like the traps afforded by it and the ability to use my best athlete to hawk the ball from the top. Because of my team's lack of height this year, I am toying with a 1-1-3/2-3 look. Choosing a zone should also include your belief in ball pressure. Is your zone going to allow the offensive guard to make the first pass? I like the ball pressured at all times in high school, because the level of play in my league is often not of the highest level. We want the unsure guard to make mistakes because of this pressure. With this pressure, the defense is

in a position to take advantage of any mistakes made. Getting points from the defense takes the pressure off the set plays we run during the game. Our defense has been a great part of our offense for years.

The Three-Point Shot

Many man defense coaches who try to plan zone often cringe when the opposition makes a three-point shot. Teams will launch three-point shots at a higher rate in most instances versus a zone. The offensive team will make some three-point shots, but if those makes are after long possessions and from people the defense wants taking them, then your zone did its job.

Rebounding

All zone defenses have trouble spots in their rebounding ability. As a coach you must be aware of those trouble spots. You must also be aware of where your zone gives you rebounding advantages. Defensive rebounding can be enhanced if routinely practiced. Players must be aware of their box-out responsibilities. They must be able to read the shot attempt and anticipate where the rebound will go.

Defending the Post

In high school, scoring from the post is the focus of many offensive sets. We focus on fronting the post player when we are in a zone defense. Many teams do not practice the lob pass to their post players. When the perimeter player sees the post fronted, he usually reverses the ball. If the lob pass is thrown, many times it is poorly executed resulting in a turnover. As a team, we practice fronting the post and the footwork associated with it. We use the swim move to get the proper position in regard to defending the post. We also practice lob passing for our centers to help them in our zone offense and also to help them learn how to defend it.

Guard Penetration to the Rim

Teaching post players not to step in and take the charge on the penetrator is always a difficult thing for me to do. I believe in the post player showing and recovering because I have found that most guards struggle finishing at the rim. Taking away the inside pass limits what the guard can do. The forward will make a higher percentage of shots than the guard will, so I always opt to make the guard finish. It is also the rare guard that can stop and pop from four to six feet in front of the rim. This rule may not always work outside of a high school setting, but it works at the high school level.

Practicing the Zone

Being able to produce from the zone takes practicing a set of rotations that every team member must habitually perform and accomplish. It is important to practice movement for all defenders. Starting with just a two-player drill, we use the centers to practice the swim move and attacking the ball in the corner.

We practice with the top three players of the 1-2-2. The slides needed for ball pressure, stopping the middle, and locating weak-side help position are practiced in a three-man shell situation. The key is the movement of the top to the fronting of the middle offensive player. The middle is the key to most zone offenses versus the 1-2-2. Either side as a result of talk covers the middle when the top is pressuring the ball. The key to the 1-2-2 is the top man. He is the best athlete on the team. This player must have the ability to get to the basket in transition off defensive steals. We use the four-man shell to improve foot movement. The five-man shell is used just to give the defenders a sense of working as a team. I also employ six, seven, and even eight offensive players versus the zone to teach the defenders how to rotate in the zone.

Trapping

Doubling or trapping the ball is a way to increase pressure. As a coach you must decide what you are going to give up if the trap is not successful. In my situation, our home court dictates that we trap in the corners because of the lack of room outside the three-point arc. As a result, we trap on all passes into the corner. On this trap we use the bottom post player and the wing to create the trap. The opposite big must swim and front the post, the top must drop and front the middle, and the opposite guard goes to the weak-side position for a rebound or to defend a lob pass. We have to spend time with our players teaching them the proper way to trap. It is worth the time to teach this. Putting defensive pressure on opposing high school athletes is a key to our success. You always want your opponents to make decisions under pressure. Poor passes and bad shot selection often result from good pressure defense.

When to Go Man

When to abandon the zone defense is always a decision that is made because you are on the wrong end of a score. Before we commit to man defense, we trap every pass. If this is unsuccessful we will call a timeout and go to man defense. The change to man should ignite my players to play a total deny defense. A problem will be that there will be no weak-side help in this defense. However, it is worth the risk if we can create turnovers by deflections and five-second violations.

Why Not Zone?

If Jim Boeheim and John Chaney can play zone defense, why can't I at the high school level? Zone defense has become my identity as a high school coach. I believe in ball pressure and forcing offensive players to make decisions in pressure situations. Most teams do not have a good zone offense. Their man offenses are usually more elaborate. Thus, we believe that zone defense has an inherent advantage over man defense.

The 2-3 Zone

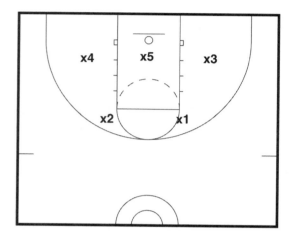

Diagram 156

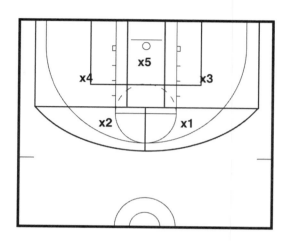

Diagram 157

Once you have made an active decision to utilize zone defense, you must now decide which defense(s) to have in your team's playbook. The most common form of zone defense is the 2-3 look.

The Basics

There are two schools of thought as far as your initial general alignment. The first (diagram 156) is a basic plan starting each defensive player at a specific point on the floor. The second (diagram 157) shows the shared responsibilities of each defensive position and theorizes that each player could begin a defensive position at any point in his/her area. This introduces the match-up concept in its most basic form; each individual defender's position is determined by the location of offensive players in their "zone."

Much like man-to-man, DO NOT allow entry of the ball into the middle, painted area. Whether by pass or by dribble, zones are most easily defeated from the inside out!

Another offensive philosophy popular when playing against the zone is to "beat the zone down the court" and not allow the defense to get set.

Diagram 156 shows a method for allowing good transition teams to dictate offensive possessions. While your players are running to their spots on the floor, the offensive players are positioning themselves to best attack. Diagram 157 shows initial match-up areas, which allow for your defensive players to learn to minimize quick-hitting offensive attacks.

Rotations must occur on the release of the pass, not any sooner or later. Do not allow a ball fake to shift your positioning. A late shift can leave a zone open to penetrating cuts and dribble. It allows the offense to reset movement and look for openings. Proper rotations allow you to always guard two offensive players with three defenders, even in cases of an overload.

Always challenge the shot and block out. With solid principles, your team should be able to contest any shot. Rebounding is a challenge for a zone; however, if proper rebound areas are taught based on shot origin, rebounding can become a positive in your zone defense. The rebounding section of this book offers a multitude of drills and teaching

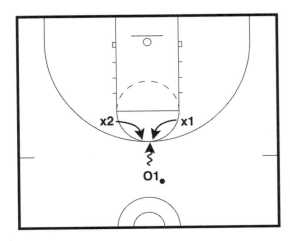

Diagram 158

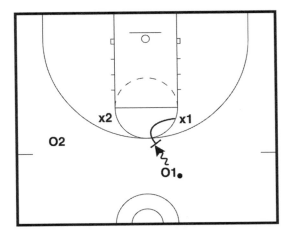

Diagram 159

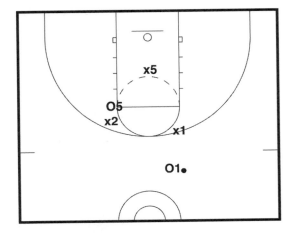

Diagram 160

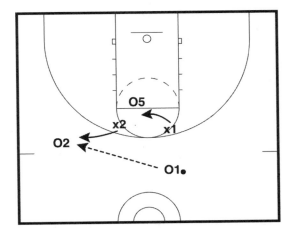

Diagram 161

tips on finishing defensive possessions with the ball in your hands.

Close out to a predetermined distance, use the three-point arc as a guide, and change this close-out range dependent upon your opponent's perimeter-shooting ability.

Rotations

The first priority in the 2-3 zone is for the top position guards to deny dribble entry to the middle of the lane. X1 and X2 must either collapse middle, touching hands and forcing O1 to the outside (diagram 158) or either defender could match up man-to-man on O1 if there is not another offensive player in his zone (diagram 159).

High post responsibility also initially falls on the top guards. They must pinch to deny entry to a high post offensive player, or they must decide

ball responsibility and high post responsibility (diagram 160). Always front the high post so the defender does not get stuck below, unable to close out on a pass to the wing. X5 will have help to the basket in event of a lob.

On a pass to the wing, the ball-side guard must close out with the weak-side guard collapsing to the foul line area, ready to match up to a high post offensive player or close out back to the point guard (diagram 161).

In some cases of ball reversal, or in cases where the offense does not have a player occupying the corner (or ball side below the foul line), it is very important that the wing defender be prepared to close out on a pass to the wing foul-line extended (diagram 162), after which the ball-side guard will bump the wing defender back down to his zone (diagram 163).

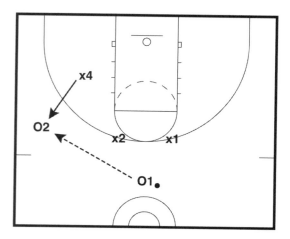

Diagram 162

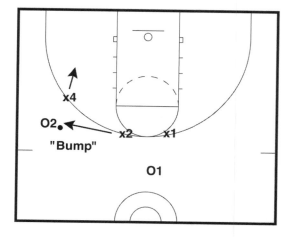

Diagram 163

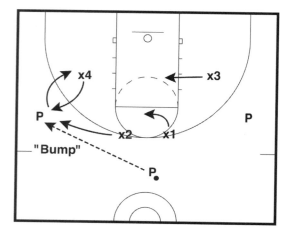

Diagram 164

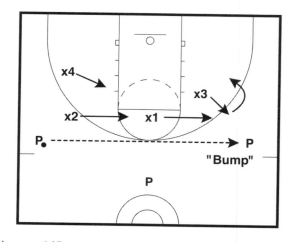

Diagram 165

This action is important to the success of your zone in contesting perimeter jump shots and preventing dribble penetration. It can be broken down and drilled easily with three passers and a shell zone of four players, two guards and two wing spots. Diagram 164 shows a point-to-wing entry with X2 bumping down X4, and diagram 165 shows a wing-to-wing skip pass where X3 initially closes out and X1 bumps him down to the baseline.

Defending the Post

In this 2-3 zone, the guards have a tremendous responsibility (which has been covered briefly to this point) in defending the high post area. Note that if this responsibility is given to the five-man, you will end up running more of a 2-1-2 defense, with less help from the wings on ball reversal. I

advise against the 2-1-2 look as it does not allow you the leniency to front the high post as we can in this 2-3 look. This allows the ball into the heart of your zone, which is number one on our list of what NOT to allow. Note: If you are looking for a zone versus a weak perimeter team, consider playing 2-3 but moving your close-out range back from the three to a midrange spot.

Diagram 166 shows a point-to-wing entry, with an offensive player in the high post. As the guard X1 and wing X3 defend the ball action on the perimeter, the guard X2 continues to front the post as he flashes across. The center defender X5 shadows O5, continuing to provide support against the lob pass, as well as preparing to bump and deny O5 if he flashes down the lane.

On the pass from the wing to the point, X2 releases from the post to guard the point, while X1

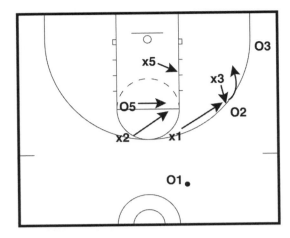

Diagram 166

Diagram 167

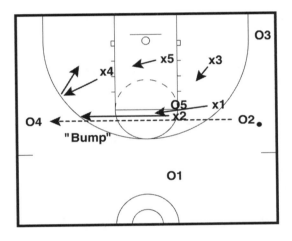

Diagram 168

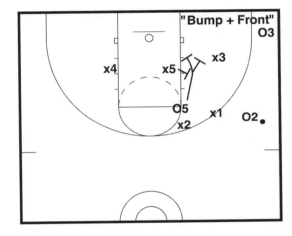

Diagram 169

moves from the wing to defend the high post (diagram 167). It is very important for X3 to shade higher to cover a potential back pass to O2 until X1 can bump him back down. On the wing-to-wing skip pass (diagram 168), X4 has initial close-out responsibility, X2 must bump him down, and X1 must sprint to defend the high post. If you can make these rotations quickly and initiate movement on the release of the ball, you can induce bad passes and deflections in an area where transition points by your guards are a certainty.

The low-post area has several concerns, as, much like any defense, a main goal of your zone is to deny the offense any easy layups or post baskets. Common offensive concepts include high-low or double post action, overloads, as well as slicing cuts by perimeter players intended to open gaps or create penetrating pass opportunities. The short

corner is a popular offensive tool that will be covered here. X5 cannot fall asleep at the wheel! As discussed, if there is an offensive player in the high post, X5 must be prepared to provide assistance in defending against the lob and any cuts to the basket.

If O5 cuts to the basket and there is no longer a high post player, X5 can front. The lob pass is one of the toughest in basketball. X5 can use the rim as another defender. X4 is on the weak side prepared to deflect any lob attempt (diagram 169).

If there is a high post offensive player, X5 would 3/4 front from the high side. Be ready to turn and defend any lob to the high post (as X1 or X2 is fronting the high post). In the event that X5 must leave a low post offensive player to defend the lob, the ball-side wing (in this case X3) must collapse-step under to defend the post (diagram 170).

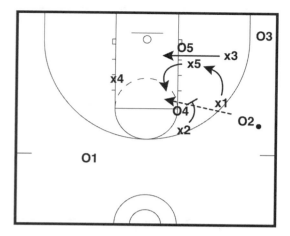

Diagram 170

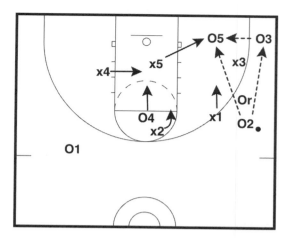

Diagram 171

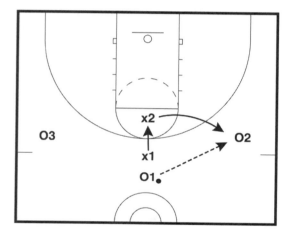

Diagram 172

X4 cannot jump to the lob, as it leaves a weak side layup opportunity open for O1.

NOTE: At this point, your best bet is to allow the ball to be kicked out to a jump shooter, rather than down to a dunker. A guard (X1 in this case) may be available to close out on a wing shooter.

X5 must front or 3/4 front the low post, because a low post entry is just as dangerous as allowing the ball to enter the middle painted area. It can lead to a post score, foul, or an easy pass to a cutter from the high post area.

NOTE: If the ball ever reaches the painted area or the post, all defenders should collapse to the ball or below the level of the ball. This forces the offense to kick out, rather than continue to attack the basket.

The Short Corner

Any pass to the short corner (diagram 171) triggers our only automatic trap. X5 and the wing defender, X3 in this case, immediately jump to the ball and initiate a trap with the baseline acting as a third defender. X1 and X2 must drop to the level of the ball, and X4 must step middle to deny or deflect any attempt at a lane cut by the offensive player from the high post area.

O5's options should be a kick back to O3, in which case X1 can close out until X3 can bump him back up, or a tough skip pass to either O2 through the trap or opposite to O1. Either pass should provide X2 a good chance of deflecting or stealing.

Decisions, Decisions

Of course, anything covered here can be manipulated to take into account your personnel, upcoming opponents and/or style of play. If you have a talented post defender, you may let him single cover a pass to the short corner, allowing you more freedom to defend possible passing lanes. With quick guards you might initiate your zone with a twist action (diagram 172), making the zone appear to be a 1-1-3 set initially and settling into a 2-3. This also denies offenses looking to utilize the high post early in their sets. You may also designate trap areas or players. This allows you to key on weaker points in an offense, as well as add a trap to disguise a weaker link in your defense. If you take this approach, the most important aspect will be the position of your secondary "help" defenders. Always keep in mind the rule of three defending two, even in the case of a trap!

Tony Staffiere
Colby College, ME

The Use and Benefits of the 1-3-1 Zone

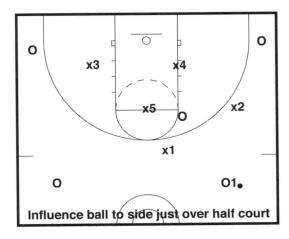

Diagram 173

Diagram 174

While many basketball theorists differ on the reasons to use a 1-3-1 half-court zone defensive alignment, most will concur that it allows coaches to provide a different defensive look to neutralize proficient three-point shooting from the wing areas and talented post players on the other team.

Of course, with any defense there are areas of vulnerability. In the 1-3-1 zone, coaches should be concerned that the ball has a tendency to find its way to the corners often against this defense. However, statistics will show shooting percentages decrease when the ball is shot from the corners of the court. This is a high-risk defense with high rewards to be gained when executed correctly.

Alignment/Slides (Diagrams 173 and 174)

X1 should be the best on-ball defender. He is responsible for influencing the ball to one side of the floor as soon as it crosses half court. He should sprint to cover the ball-side elbow area when the ball is in the corner. This player could also be your best scorer as he will get out ahead in transition quite often.

X2 and X3 are wing players. They are responsible for the left and right sidelines. They must remember to keep their outside feet as close to the sideline as possible. X2 and X3 must funnel the ball back to the middle and not allow any direct passes to the corners. They must sprint to the back-side block when the ball is on the opposite side of the floor. (diagram 175 and 176)

X4 should be the most athletic/fastest player side-to-side. This spot should be played by your point guard in most situations. This player must be able to cover ground from corner to corner on any ball reversal. He will start on the ball-side block as the ball crosses half court. X4 will extend his slide out to cover the ball in the corner. He must be aware of the ball at all times and act much like a free-safety in football.

X5 should be the tallest post player. He is responsible for keeping the ball out of the painted area. X5 will become the last line of defense and

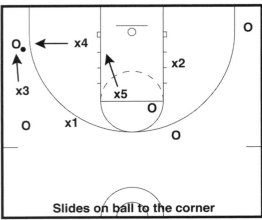

Slides on ball to the corner

Diagram 175

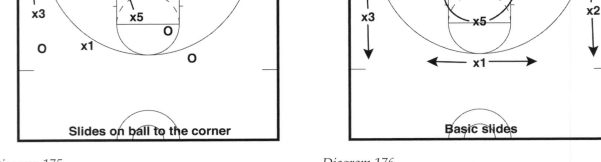

Basic slides

Diagram 176

step up on any ball penetration to the painted area. He is not necessarily assigned to a player in an area and should key the movement of the ball at all times.

Keys

Point and baseline defenders are connected on a line and slide in a side-to-side pattern. The wing defenders are also connected on a line and slide in an up-and-down pattern. It is a good idea to have your point guard play the baseline spot, as he is usually the first player back in defensive transition situations.

The point defender must pick up the ball immediately as it crosses half court and influence the ball to a specific side of the floor. This player should be a primary scorer as he will get chances to get out ahead in offensive transition.

Wing players can never be too wide in their initial alignment, so as not to allow a direct pass to the corner. When one wing player is playing the ball on his side, the other sprints to the opposite

block and vice versa. The middle defender must keep the ball out of the painted area. He should be reminded to key the ball at all times and not be concerned with defending a specific offensive player.

Changing the Look

The best way to use the 1-3-1 half-court zone defense is to show different variations of it throughout the course of the game. For example, you could call two different 1-3-1 zone patterns in a game. The first is a more passive style called "soft," where players slide in the traditional patterns as diagrammed, influencing the ball from sideline to sideline with no trapping of the ball involved. The other pattern, called "hard," would involve patterns trapping designated areas of the floor such as the corner or the sideline. The players involved in trapping the corners would be X2/X3 and X4. The players involved in trapping the sideline would be X2/X3 and X1.

Part Five:
Full-Court
Pressure Defense

A Pressing Philosophy

Teams that are committed to pressing need to determine what their pressing philosophy will be. For coaches that commit to pressing 75% of the game or more, I recommend that you consider "the press" to accomplish all your full-court pressure goals.

There are endless resources for types of full-court pressing schemes. This section is dedicated to the philosophy and organization of "the press." Rick Pitino's white-and-black press deserves full credit and is the backbone of the press. It is recommended that you master the following full-court press alignments and their reference colors.

- 1-2-1-1 full-court press—black
- 2-2-1 3/4 court press—white
- Man-to-man full court (no trap)—red
- Man-to-man full court (run and jump, trap)—blue
- Box-and-one full-court press—gold

Rick Pitino's black-an-white press utilizes the fundamental concept of box-diamond. The box-diamond concept is essential to the success of your 1-2-1-1 and 2-2-1 presses. The simple definition of box-diamond is that when the ball is guarded in the middle of the floor, the four players are up in the press in a diamond, and when the ball is on the sideline, the four players are in a box. The box and diamond will be distorted because it is a match-up press and will take the form of the press offense. Mastering the box-diamond theory is the key to pressing successfully. It should be drilled every day. After establishing an effective box-diamond press, the man-to-man and box-and-one can be added. Build your pressure defense starting with box-diamond and add from there.

Why Press?
- Establishes superior conditioning

- Changes tempo (slower and faster tempo)
- Forces turnovers
- Creates easy baskets
- Encourages aggressive mentality
- Develops team depth
- Improves teams press offense
- Eliminates early offensive, secondary break and quick-hitting plays
- Disrupts set plays and continuity offenses
- Puts offense deep into the shot clock
- Takes advantage of poor ball handling and poor press attacks

The Press

The press is a philosophy of combining multiple full-court defensive looks in a fast-paced, changing defensive environment. The element of surprise and the ability to disguise full-court pressure is the essence of the press. Once the box-diamond concepts are developed and man-to-man concepts are added, the press truly begins to evolve.

The coach will say, "Get in the press." The team needs to react and be on the same page. Some teams are always in the press, so the particular press we are executing needs to be communicated. The use of verbal calls or colored sheets of paper on the bench directs the team as to the specific press that is to be used. The type of press used can be determined based on what occurs on the offensive possession. For example, the pressing team gets into a 1-2-1-1 (black) after a made lay-up and made free throws. After made perimeter jump shots or on dead-ball possessions, the press can be 2-2-1 (white). Man-to-man full-court (red) can be utilized in all special situations and dead balls and man-to-man full-court trap (blue) and box-and-one full court (gold) can be effective after time-outs. It is up to the coach to determine which cues will be used to direct the press.

Changing full-court pressure defenses will keep the offensive team on their heels and create doubt and confusion. It will cause them to play faster and take them out of their comfort zone. It will not be uncommon to hear the offensive team saying, "What are they in?" The press will cause opposing teams to spend significant time preparing for your full-cover pressure, taking away from preparing in other areas.

The press is an aggressive game plan. It gives your team an aggressive personality and gives the players a full-court pressure mentality and philosophy to be proud of. It becomes a big part of your team's identity and culture.

When the press is at its best, it is a beautiful weapon. The collaboration of the team on the floor with the coaching staff and the bench creates togetherness that supports team-building. The bench's contribution is essential to the press. Their enthusiasm fuels the defense and, since many of them will be substituted into the game at some point, it helps the bench be ready and prepared. All of the little things are extremely important in becoming a successful pressing team.

How It Works

Depending on your coaching style and the strengths and weaknesses of your opponents, you will create a pressing game plan. Some games you may start in a press, other games you may hold the press until later in the first half or even hold until the second half. Starting the game in the press allows you to evaluate the other team's press attack. The press offense used is usually "as practiced" the first few times they run it, so it will give you a chance to diagram their pattern and make adjustments. You can choose the type of press depending on their alignment.

One of the first things you look for in a press offense is who is taking the ball out of bounds. Is it a forward/center or a guard? Is it the point guard? All of these questions will help determine your press package for that game. With the use of advance scouting, you may be able to determine this prior to tip-off.

Your game plan may be to start the game in 1-2-1-1 (black) after made baskets and dead balls, man-to-man full-court with no trap (red) after missed shots and free throws, and 2-2-1 (white) after made free throws. Add the man-to man run and jump

after time outs. The box-and-one (gold) can be used if a dominant offensive player needs to be shut down. You can keep the ball out of the player's hands early in the possession and wear him down. This press (gold) is great to use after time outs. Many coaches will spend the entire time out drawing a play for the best player to score. Players need to communicate. They need to talk and point all the time. They need to be reminding each other that they are in black, white, red, etc.

Box-and-One Full-Court Press (Gold)

The box-and-one full-court press (gold) can be very effective. You can run it in either straight man-to-man or use the box-diamond concepts. Either way, the defense is designed to faceguard the player that you do not want to catch the ball. Most of the time the offensive team's center is out of the press offense. Therefore, the press will take place three-on-three. Box-diamond concepts are in play although the box and diamond will be severely distorted. If the offense gets the center involved in the press offense, the press can be more box-diamond, utilizing the center as the fourth player up in the press. In the event that the man that we are denying catches the ball, the other three players work with the ball handler in box-diamond concepts with the center covering the basket. If you choose to go straight man-to-man, there are opportunities to switch, run and jump and trap.

Hustle Plays

Doing the little things—the hustle plays—will ultimately be the most important part of the press. Charting these behaviors and actions in practice and games with a reward system will train your team in the importance of doing these intangibles. Listed below are many of the little things.

- Making layups (scoring allows the team to set up the press)
- Challenging every shot
- Communicating and pointing
- Jamming the rebounder
- Playing hard, tough and aggressive without fouling
- Gathering deflections
- Working to get five-second and 10-second count violations
- Relentless back-tipping at all times
- Shot-blocking presence

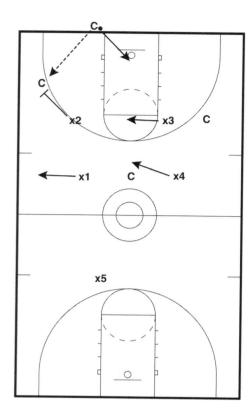

Diagram 177

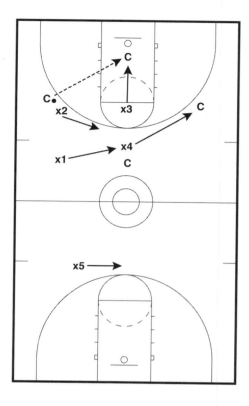

Diagram 178

- Creating steals
- Taking charges all over the court
- Diving on the floor for loose balls
- Sprinting out of traps

Essential Press Drills

Box-diamond drill (2-2-1)

When the ball is out of bounds, the four players are matched up in a box. X2 is applying hard ball pressure. The other three defenders are playing off in help position. When the ball is passed to the side, the defenders are still in a box (although distorted). When the ball is on the sideline the defense is in a box. This drill starts in a 3-2-1 alignment (diagram 177).

X2 is pressuring the ball, looking to force a speed or uncontrolled dribble up the sideline. The ball is on the side; therefore, the four players are in a box. X4 is denying the pass to the middle. When the ball is passed back to the middle, the defense will move into a diamond (diagram 178).

The ball is in the middle, so the four defenders are in a diamond. X3 is pressuring the ball. X4 and X2 are in support. X1 is in an open stance cover-

ing the middle. X4 is slow out of the middle and X1 is quick into the middle (diagram 179).

The ball is reversed. The ball is now on the sideline, so the defense is in a box. X4 is pressuring the ball. X1 is covering the sideline. X2 has the middle. X3 has dropped. Once again, X1 is slow out of the middle and X2 is quick into the middle. When the ball is on the sideline, the middle is being denied (full fronted, diagram 180).

Box-diamond drill (1-2-1-1)

Players start in the 1-2-1-1 alignment. X4 pressures the ball, looking for a five-second count. X2 forces the offensive player to the corner. If the ball is entered below the block, there is an automatic trap. If the ball is entered above the block, there is no trap and X4 drops back into a box. We are then in a box-diamond (diagram 181).

X2 and X4 trap the ball. X1 has the sideline and iddle. X3 has the sideline and middle. X3 is anticipating taking the next pass. (X4 can play two passes in a row if the trap and pass are close enough.) This is desired but can't always happen if the offensive spacing is good (diagram 182).

The ball is in the middle; therefore, the four press players are in a diamond. X1 has a long slide. That

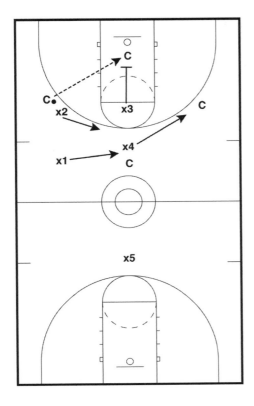

Diagram 179

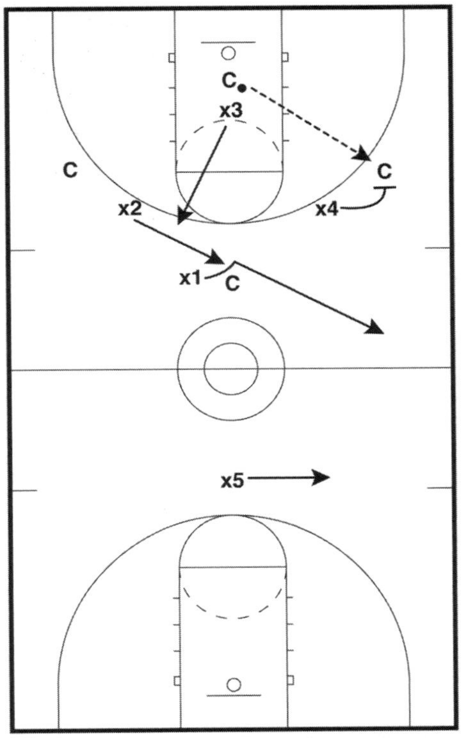

Diagram 180

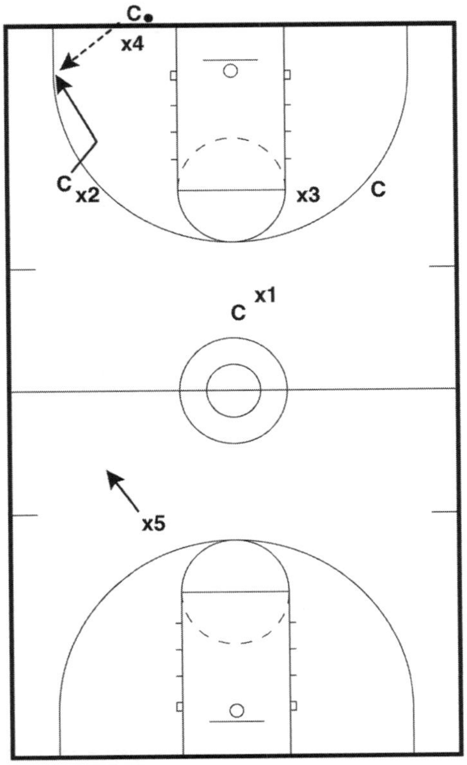

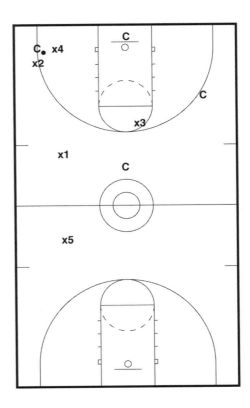

Diagram 181

Diagram 182

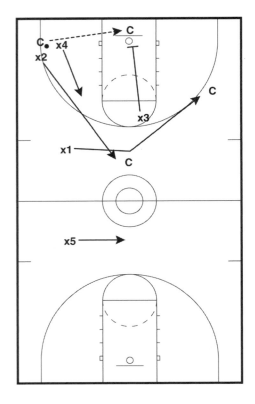

Diagram 183

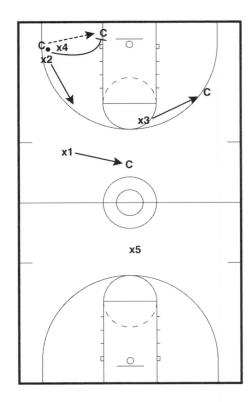

Diagram 184

is one of the reasons he, our quickest player, is in the back (diagram 183).

X4 can play two passes in a row if the distance between the pass back is close enough. The ball is in the middle, so the four press defenders have moved into a diamond (diagram 184).

Trap rotations

X2 and X3 force a low entry (diagram 185). Four defenders form a box (diagram 186). X2 forces the dribbler into a speed or uncontrolled dribble up the sideline. X1 looks to level the ball and trap. X4 covers the sideline. X3 covers the middle (diagram 187).

If the ball is thrown over head, turn and retrap with X4. Sprinting out of traps is very improtant. X2 sprints out of the trap and covers the middle. X3 covers the weak-side elbow (diagram 188).

If the ball is thrown over the second trap and O2 (offensive player in the corner) is not a shooter, the press is off and X4 can play two passes in a row. X3 covers the weak-side block, X2 covers the high post and X1 sprints out of the trap to cover the strong -side elbow (diagram 189).

If O2 is a shooter, you may want to make the decision to "bring X5 out." If X5 goes out, X3 cov-

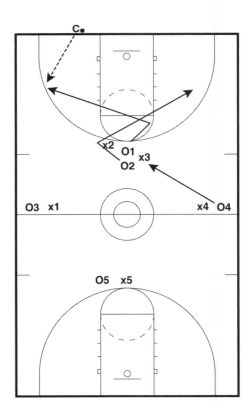

Diagram 185

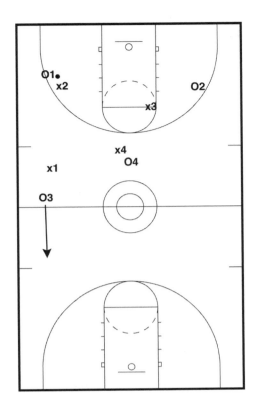

Diagram 186

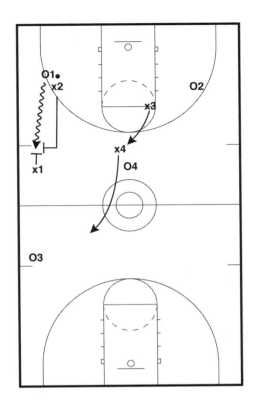

Diagram 187

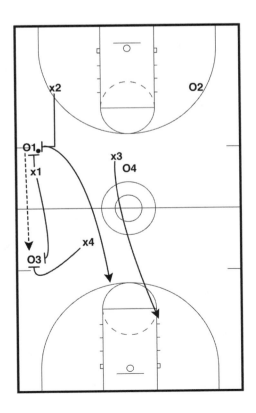

Diagram 188

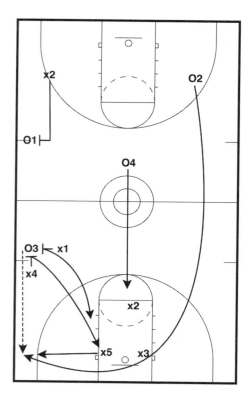

Diagram 189

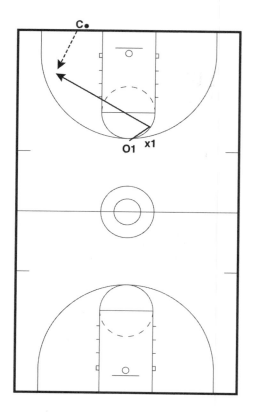

Diagram 190

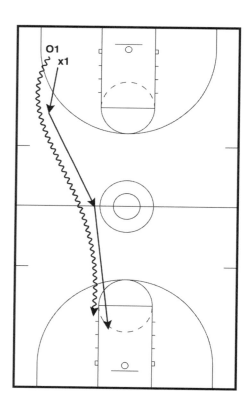

Diagram 191

ers the strong-side black until X4 gets to the low post. Most teams will call the press off after two traps (diagram 189).

One-on-one full court

The offensive player starts at the desired press offensive alignment location. X1 uses an open stance and pushes the offensive player to the corner. He only goes for a steal if it is 100% guaranteed. X1 is trying the force a low entry below the black (diagram 190).

X1 is guarding the ball fullcourt. The offensive layer is looking coast-to-coast to score. This is not a zig zag drill. The offensive is looking to blow by the defender and score. X1 is looking to level the ball and turn the ball handler and not allow a layup. Look to force a contested jump shot (diagram 191).

Back tip drill one-on-one

Choose two players of similar speed and ball-handling skills. One player lines up above the block. The other lines up on the elbow. When the coach says "go," the player above the block throws the ball to the plyaer at the elbow. If the back tipper cannot get close to the ball handler, shorten

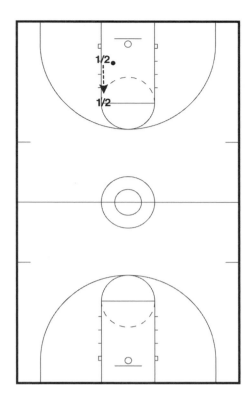

Diagram 192

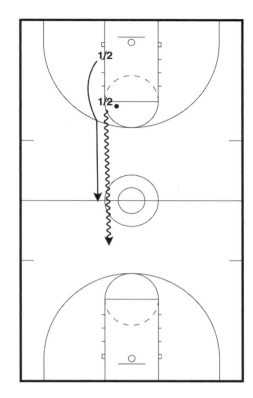

Diagram 193

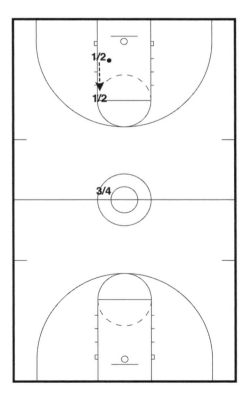

Diagram 194

the distance between the passer and the dribbler (diagram 192).

The player at the elbow that received the pass dribbles full speed with the outside hand (the right as shown in this diagram). The dribbler cannot cross over or change hands. The passer sprints from behind, trying to tip the ball from behind. He uses his inside hand (left as shown in the diagram) to reach. Tell players to "run through the ball." Put cones in the middle of the floor to reduce the playing area. The dribbler tries to go coast-to-coast and lay the ball in (diagram 193).

Back tip drill one-versus-two

This is the same set up as the Back Tip Drill One-on-One except that we add another player at the half court aligned with the ball. This player could be a different position player. The player below the block passes to the player at the elbow (diagram 194).

The player with the ball speed dribbles with the intention of going coast-to-coast for a layup. The dribbler can change hands with the dribble, but the court is still cut in half. The defensive player at the half court moves to the level of the ball or slows the ball down. The back tipper is sprinting.

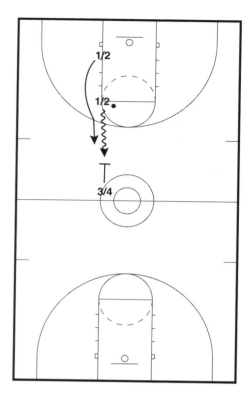

Diagram 195

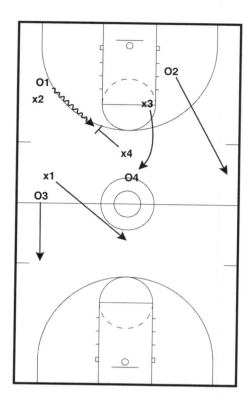

Diagram 196

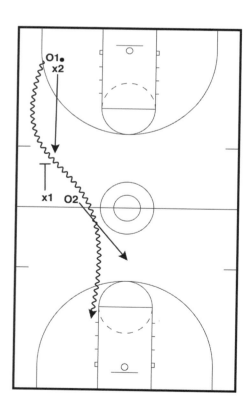

Diagram 197

The plan is to get the dribbler to slow up enough for the tipper to get to the ball (diagram 195).

Middle back tip drill

When the dribbler beats the defender to the middle of the floor, the back tip takes place. X4 steps up to the level of the ball. X4 is buying time for X2, who was beaten to catch up and tip the ball from behind. X3 and X1 have to get below the ball and cover open areas (diagram 196).

Two-on-two full court

Starts the same as the one-on-one full court. The offensive player starts at the desired press offensive alignment location. X2 uses an open stance and pushes the offensive player to the corner. X1 is in the back of the press, looking to level the ball. X2 can back tip, X1 and X2 can trap or switch (diagram 197).

If there is not enough ball pressure, the ball handler often throws the ball over the top for a layup. If this is a problem, you can tell your player that he can't lob over the top. The point is that the ball handler shouldn't be able to see the receiver and is under so much pressure that the pass can't be made. Players play 2-on-2 half court when tran-

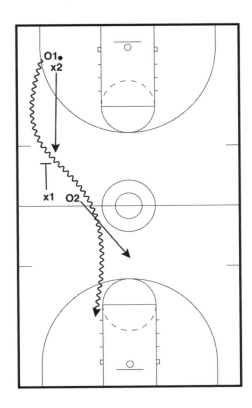

Diagram 198

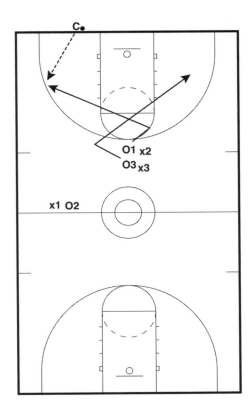

Diagram 199

sition is stopped. Once again, the defense is looking to force a contested jump shot and not a layup (diagram 198).

Three-on-three full-court box-diamond

This drill builds up from the two-on-two. Add a third guard to the play. Start them in any press alignment. In this alignment, it is OK to switch when they cross. Both X2 and X3 are looking to force a low entry or get a steal. A five-second count is desired as well (diagram 199).

The ball is entered on the sideline. Defensive players are in a box (missing the fourth player). Play three-on-three full court. Players are looking for back tips, steals, traps and switches. They should also look to force contested shots. No layups (diagram 200)!

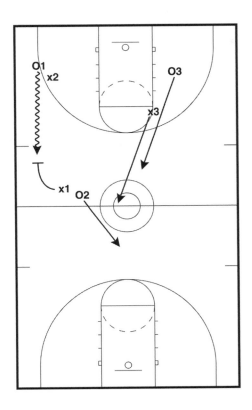

Diagram 200

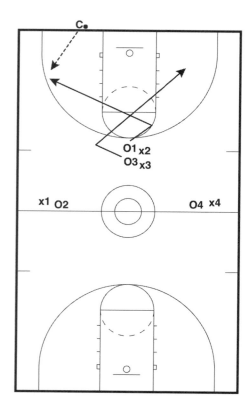

Diagram 201

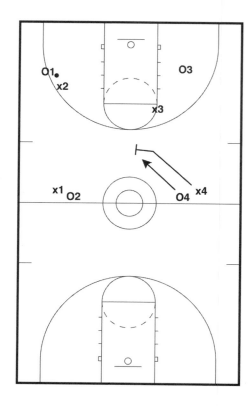

Diagram 202

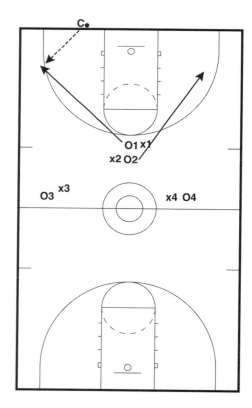

Diagram 203

Four-on-four full-court box-diamond

The play builds up from a three-on-three. Add a fourth player (a four-man) to the play. Start in any press alignment. In this alignment, it is OK to switch when they cross. Both X2 and X3 are looking to force a low entry or get a steal. A five-second count is desired (diagram 201).

The ball is entered on the sideline. The defensive players are in a box. If the offensive four flashes to the middle, the defense denies the flash. The defense is still in a box; it is just distorted. The box-diamond is a match-up press, so it will take the form of the offense. Play four-on-four full court. Look for back tips, steals, traps and switches. Look to force contested shots. No layups (diagram 202)!

Run and jump drill

The drill begins with the four defenders matching up with the offense man-to-man (diagram 203).

X1 forces and funnels player O1 up the sideline or gets O1 to zigzag and turn back. X3 leaves O3 and looks to level the ball or trap. If O1 picks up the dribble or turns his back, there should be a trap. If not, there should be a jump-switch. X1

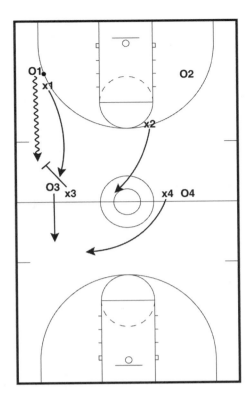

Diagram 204

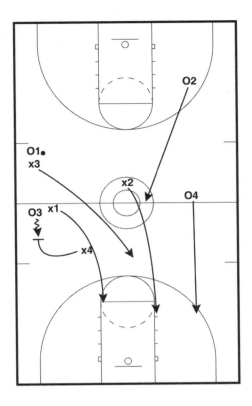

Diagram 205

should switch to cover O3. X2 and X4 move into support positions similar to trap rotations (diagram 204).

X4 and X1 can run and jump. X3 and X2 are in support (diagram 205).

Five-on-five press game

The five-on-five press game is played full court starting with a jump ball. It is played using the game clock, for example 16 minutes. Play eight minutes of 2-2-1 and eight minutes of 1-2-1-1 or use your cues to set the particular press. A layup by a big equals 1-2-1-1 (black), a layup by a guard equals man-to-man no trap (red), a three-point shot equals 2-2-1 (white). Game rules apply. The scoring is based on defensive stops and hustle points. You are rewarded by scoring because you get to get in the press. You can add and remove categories based on your team's points of emphasis.

The scoring is as follows:
- Defensive stops: 2 points
- Deflection: 1 point
- Forcing turnover: 1 point
- Blocked shots: 1 point

- Steal: 1 point
- Take charge: 3 points
- Dive on the floor to recover ball: 1 point

You lose points by:
- Not challenging shots: -1 point
- Not back tipping: -1 points
- Turnovers: -1 point
- Bad shots: -1 point
- Not blocking out: -1 point
- Giving up "O" rebound: -1 point
- Fouling: -1 point

Trapping Philosophy

Trapping in the press is random. It is not designated, which makes it very difficult to scout and prepare for. It is difficult for the offense to know when a trap is occurring, and the threat is always there. For example, in the 1-2-1-1 a trap always occurs when the offense enters the ball below the block in the corner. If the ball is entered above the block, there is not a trap and the press moves to a 2-2-1 alignment. Traps occur when a ball handler is in an uncontrolled dribble or speed dribble. If he spins, turns his back or picks up his dribble, traps can take place.

Back Tipping

Backtipping is an essential part of the press which enables the defender to avoid being beaten by the dribbler. Running from behind and tipping causes the dribbler to hear footsteps which cause fear. The back tip drill teaches defenders that they CAN get the ball. Sometimes it's just a fingernail that touches the ball. Regardless of whether you fully tip the ball, pressure from behind is very effective because the ball handler is worried about what is ahead. In addition, teams that are constantly back tipping are always sprinting to get below the ball. Players in the press are always getting back on defense.

Fear and Panic

The press is engineered to inflict fear into the offensive team. Defensive players guarding the ball try to take away vision, create a speed or uncontrolled dribble and take away free thinking time. These tactics add up and create panic in the offensive team. Combined with fatigue, fear can create disarray within a team and with their coaches. During the confusion, the defensive team is pressing and stealing the ball, creating high-percentage layups.

Risk Versus Reward

The press is a conservative full-court pressure defense. It is designed to NOT give up layups or uncontested three-point shots. That does not mean that it will not force turnovers, cause fatigue and change tempo—it will. The press attempts to get the offensive team to throw the ball away rather than to steal the ball. Players need to understand risk versus reward. They need to understand that they are playing hard and aggressively, but smart and technically sound. Many presses are designed to steal the ball immediately when it is entered. While that happens at times, most of the steals come at half court as interceptions or back tips. In football terms, we get more interceptions than sacks. The rotations and slides ensure that the basket is covered and layups are not given up. Many presses give up layups because they end after the first trap or half court. The press uses full-court slides that keep the basket defended at all times.

Substitution Patterns

The press requires at least nine players, well-conditioned and fully schooled in the defensive philosophy. Frequent substitution is a key element to successful pressing. Fresh bodies are vital, and players must be playing hard at all times. They must sprint. Players should never rest on the floor. If they are tired, they must come out of the game. Substituting on dead balls is essential in order to stop the clock and set the press.

Substituting with 16 minutes left in the first half for a guard (preferably your point guard) is a great strategy. If the press allows you to get an early lead and you have a great defender and press player on the bench, this substitution will allow you to rest your point guard while the press is at its best. This move will ultimately wear down the opposing team's point guard or make them substitute the back-up point guard that will struggle against pressure.

The Center

Your center must be able to change between on-the-ball in the 1-2-1-1 (black) and the last line of defense in the 2-2-1 (white). It helps if your center is active and has good instincts. There are situations in the back of the press where decision-making is vital. Should he commit to the steal, block the shot or stay home? When teaching the press it may appear that the center is not involved, because the center is not utilized in the box-diamond. It is essential that the center understands a box-diamond. It is the responsibility of the center to direct the press. The center sees the whole press in front of him. He can communicate and direct the press from behind. Centers that can communicate and point will help the defense adjust with commands.

Athleticism and Quickness

Many critics of full-court pressing feel that athletes and quickness are the only reasons presses are successful. Teams that have superior quickness can make the press a lethal weapon. But I would not discourage you from instituting the press with some less athletic and slower players. If the player has great anticipations skills, a high basketball IQ and understands the press, he can be effective. Because the changing looks of the press will slow down and confuse the offense, its neutralizes that speed disadvantage. Players that understand where to move can be very good in the press, and their lack of speed will not break down defense.

Early Season Victories

Teams can win games early in the season on the simple fact that they press. It takes time for teams to be proficient in press offense. Facing full-court pressure defense in practice is nothing like seeing it for real in a game situation. There is usually a weak link in the team's press offense. It may be a young player that is gaining experience, or it could be a veteran player that is experiencing this type of pressure for the first time. Either way, coaches learn early in the season which players need to be on the floor when facing pressure. This is a lesson the coach learns from playing against (and losing) to a pressing team.

Conclusion

In an article written in *The New Yorker* magazine by Malcolm Gladwell, author of *The Tipping Point*, *Blink* and *Outliers*, Gladwell explained why full-court pressure defenses allow the underdog to be victorious. He explains that the theory is why David beat Goliath. Whether you agree or disagree with Gladwell, he argues a good point that an aggressive game plan can neutralize an opponent's advantage.

It is my hope that you can design a pressing package that allows your team to disrupt the offense, cause fatigue, force turnovers, and not give up lay-ups or open three-point shots. If you have less athletic players that are smart, give it a try—you will be surprised. If you have a quick and athletic team, commit to the time to teach the whole press from beginning to end. Be disciplined with the slides in order not to give up layups. Change pressing defenses and put fear in your opponent. This will be the difference between making the tournament and winning the tournament.

Tony Martin
The John Carroll School, MD

Gold: A 1-2-1-1 Full-Court Zone Pressure Defense

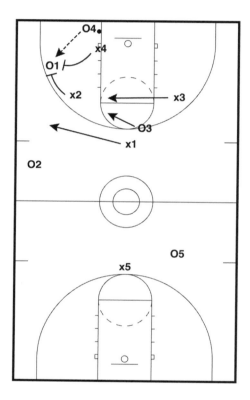

Diagram 206

This full-court press is designed for trapping and stealing the ball from opponents. It is a kamikaze defense that required quickness, hustle and much frenetic activity.

Rules and Placement of Defenders

The X4 man puts the pressure on the inbounds pass yelling "ball" (diagram 206). He must leave his feet. He shades to his inside leg with his hands in the air, encouraging a bounce pass to the short corner of the floor. Once a pass is made below the foul line/foul-line extended, X4 traps player O2 or O3 with a wind. If the ball gets to the middle of floor past the trap, X4 looks to tip the ball with his inside hand. On the tip from behind, it is important that the defender chase the ball and not the man. He works with the interceptor to slow the ball down. If the opponent likes to inbound the ball quickly, X4 must get under the basket and let the ball hit off his shoulder. Bump or get in the way of the inbounder. If the opponent likes to inbound in a more organized fashion, hand the ball quickly to the inbounder.

The X2 man is responsible for the first offensive player he sees on his side of the court below the top of the key extended. If no one is there he will back up until someone comes in his field of vision. Player X2 must not play air—he must find an offensive player and cover them. Player X2 must mirror the sideline and force the offensive player up and down the sideline. Player X2 must not let the offensive player go through him. On the catch, X2 will get close enough to get his legs into the back of his opponent's legs to prevent a sideline pivot. On a catch, X2 will establish a trap with X4. He will angle the dribbler to the sideline but do not give up the lane. If the ball is passed back to the inbounder, X2 angles to the middle of the floor, sprinting back into the passing lane.

The X3 man does the same as the X2 man but on the X3 man's side of the court. On a catch, X3 must establish a trap with X4. If a pass is made to the opposite corner, he angles to the middle of the floor until he sees the closest man on the opposite side of the floor. First look is the pass back to the inbounder. Player X3 plays helpside defense. Player X3 must get low in a crouch. He has a tough job in covering two players, but it must be done. Player X3 must gamble. He will be in the passing lane off the ball. On the long corner pass, X3 will attack the passing lane, not the man. Player X3 must not deny the pass or gamble too early. If the pass is made back to the inbound passer, X3 sprints back into the passing lane. If playing against a very patient offensive team, start the game by having X3 take away the return pass to the inbounder. This will force a quicker tempo. If the pass does not come right away, X3 will shade to the middle for secondary look.

The X1 man is the midcourt interceptor. He plays first pass over the trap and must sprint from sideline to sideline with the movement of the ball. His primary look is directly up the sideline, and his secondary look is the high-post flash to the middle. If the ball gets to the middle of the floor, he must get his nose on the ball and stop or slow its progress. This will allow X2, X3, and X4 to sprint to the paint. Player X1 never traps. If the opponent runs the inbounder through with a cut, X1 must pick him up, looking to draw a charge. Player X5 will shade the area player 1 leaves.

The X5 man plays opposite the interceptor, and his position depends on the offensive alignment. Player X5 will respect the moves down court, but he does not necessarily cover them. He must protect the basket against layups. Player X5 must discourage any midcourt passes. On any sideline pass, he must sprint straight back to the basket.

If the defense is beaten, everyone sprints back to the paint and gets into a half-court defense that has already been determined. We do not want our defenders to challenge the ball in the midcourt area. In transition defense, "accidentally" run into the opponent who has rebounding position if a shot goes up.

This defense can be used as a one-trap-only press or a multiple trap press. Everyone knows their responsibilities. Anyone not involved in a trap must look into the trap. Interceptors always have a primary and secondary look. If the ball is thrown over the top, everyone springs back and looks for the tip from behind. As soon as a pass is made out of the trap and over the trappers, the men in the first trap or any trap go back level with or in front of the ball. Now we are almost in a man-to-man defense. If the pass out of the trap is backward, we are still in our zone press.

If you have better players than your opponents, the press will create more possessions, which is an advantage. If a team beats the press but cannot get a layup, nothing bad has happened. At times one of my players might ask, "How can I cover two?" My response is simple, "If you want to play on Friday, you better figure it out." It is important to realize that someone will always be open versus the trap, but can the offense make the play?

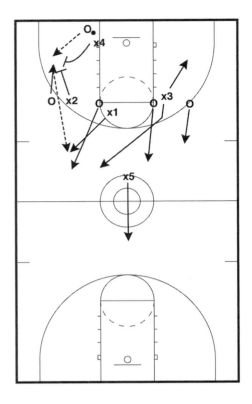

Diagram 207

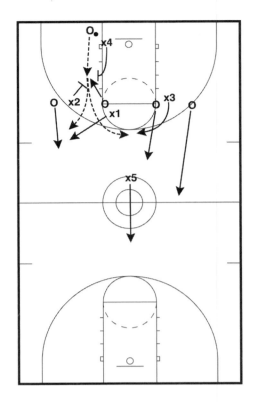

Diagram 208

Adjustments to the Press

If you are unable to get the short corner trap, and the opponent walks the ball up, look to change into a 3/4- or 1/2-court pressure. If your press gets beaten early, change presses but don't take it off.

The 1-4 inbounds set will cause match-up problems for the 1-2-1-1. Call "jam" and then adjust. You will look like you are in 1-3-1 defense, but follow the same rules as explained above. Player X4 will cover the inbounder and try to trap in the corner. Player X2 covers his side while X3 covers the opposite side and middle. If the ball goes to X3's side, then X2 has to worry about middle and ball reversal to the inbounder. Player 1 is the interceptor. Player X5 is deep (diagrams 207 and 208).

Against a 1-2-2 inbounds set we play a switching man-to-man on all crosses and screens. We must communicate well to let our teammates know what we are doing. If X5 has two men long, he must call X1 for help (diagram 209).

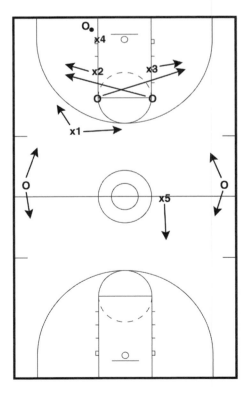

Diagram 209

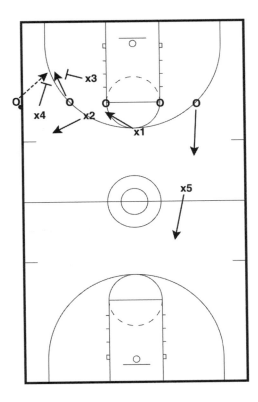

Diagram 210

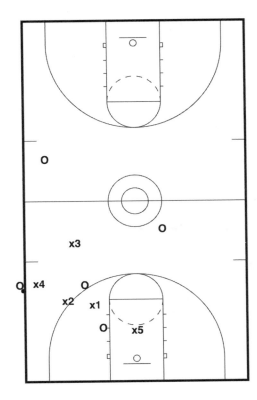

Diagram 211

With the ball in the back court (diagram 210), put X4 on the sideline where the ball is being inbounded. Turn the press around, i.e., have it face the ball-side sideline with X3 on the baseline side and X2 on the half-court side. Player X5 will be leaning toward the opposite sideline. Player X1 will be responsible for any breakouts. Player X5 should also have deep responsibility.

With the ball in the front court, be careful of the direct pass out of bounds into the post area. If the offensive team successfully throws the ball into the back court and beats your pressure, then switch into a different type of pressure (diagram 211).

Steve Treffiletti
Central Connecticut State University

Vegas: Another Look at the 1-2-1-1

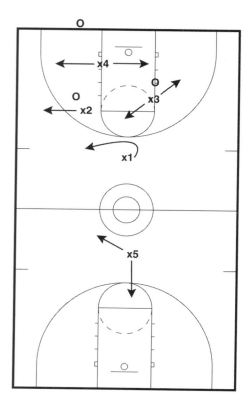

Diagram 212

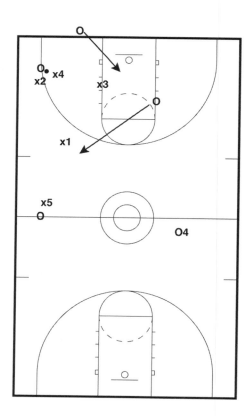

Diagram 213

The golden rule to this play: Whenever you think you are in proper defensive position, take two steps up and get closer to the ball.

Positions and Assignments

Put X4 on the inbounder (diagram 212). He should be the best overall athlete on the floor. However, we want a bigger defender to play this position. The prototype defender would be the 6'5" forward that can run and jump. He should be active and energetic. X2 must be a very good defender. He must be able to know how to force the offense into the corner, setting up a trap situation. X3 can be the other guard. This is the spot for any defensive liability. X1 is the interceptor. He must have instincts

for the ball. He is the most important part of the success of this pressure defense. X5 is the problem solver. He must try to read and react to deep passes. Typically he is the biggest and slowest of this group.

First Trap

Players X4 and X2 will bait or direct the ball to the ball-side corner (diagram 213). They will trap the ball hard. The key is to have enough pressure applied that the long diagonal skip pass is not made, but not enough pressure to get beaten up the sideline or to split the trap.

Player X3 must look to stop ball reversal to the inbounder after the trap is initiated on the ball side. He is the key to the rotation since most teams look

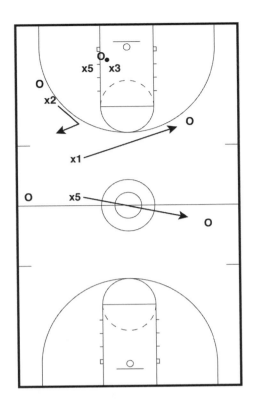

Diagram 214

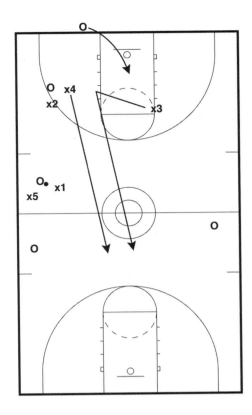

Diagram 215

to pass back to the inbounder. X1 as the interceptor is looking for any lob or floating passes to get, but he must look down the middle as well. X5 should be at least as high as the deepest man. If the offense extends and stretches the defense, X5 has deep responsibility.

If the Ball Is Reversed Back to the Inbounder

Players X3 and X5 apply the next hard, aggressive trap, allowing teammates time to get in proper position (diagram 214). The interceptor, X1, must hustle back to the middle and read the ball, trying to steal the next pass. X5 reads the play, leaving the farthest offensive player away from the ball and trying to steal any deep pass. X2 continues roaming his area.

If the Ball Is Advanced up the Sideline

Players X1 and X5 must come together for a hard, aggressive trap using the sideline as an extra defender (diagram 215). X3, X2 and X4 must hustle back to get in front of the ball, back-tapping any dribbler they come up behind. X1 and X5 must not allow the ball out of the trap. This will allow the other three defenders time to get back (diagram 216).

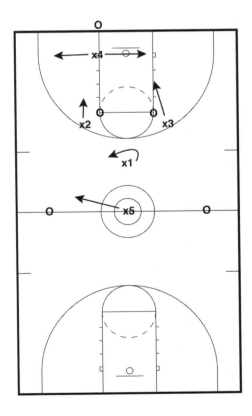

Diagram 216

2-2-1 Zone Press

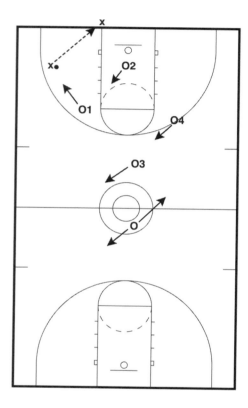

Diagram 217

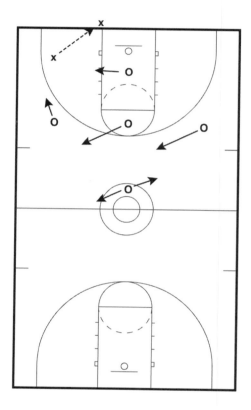

Diagram 218

Introduction

The 2-2-1 is my favorite press. It does not matter what other press you run—after the first inbound pass has been made, that zone press realigns itself and becomes a 2-2-1. You can realign from a diamond-and-one press (i.e., 1-2-1-1) after the first entry pass into the 2-2-1 (diagram 217). You can realign from a 1-3-1 press into the 2-2-1 (diagram 218).

Breakdown Drills to Build up to the 2-2-1 Press

One-versus-one: hatchet man

When the coach blows his whistle, the offensive player with the ball must attempt to beat the defense to half court (diagram 219). When the coach blows his whistle, the offensive player must leave his man and defend the next dribbler in the line (diagram 220).

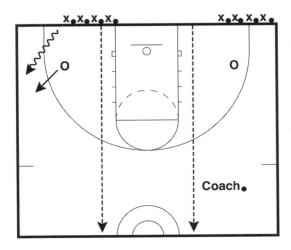

Diagram 219

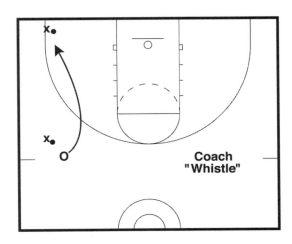

Diagram 220

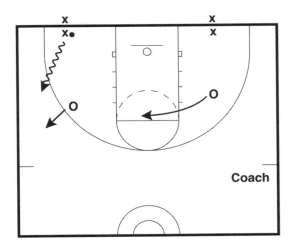

Diagram 221

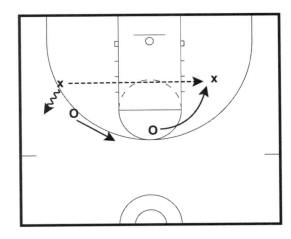

Diagram 222

Two-versus-two containment drill

We now have the front line of the press—the key is for the defender to keep the ball out of the middle. Random trapping is allowed, but the player who is not guarding the ball must play "centerfield." If the ball handler passes the ball back to the other offensive player, then the defensive roles are reversed (diagrams 221 and 222).

Four-versus-three: trap and intercept

We have four trappers, (defenders) against three attackers (offensive players). The trappers at the front do exactly the same as above (diagram 223), but when X2 receives the ball, O2 must push him to the side. O1 plays centerfield. O4 looks for a random trap if the dribbler is out of control. O3 must come over and cover X3 and try to intercept any pass attempt to him, otherwise the press will be broken (diagram 224).

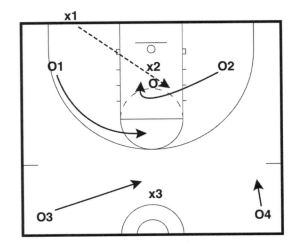

Diagram 223

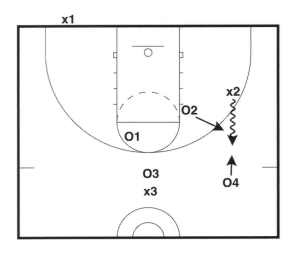

Diagram 224

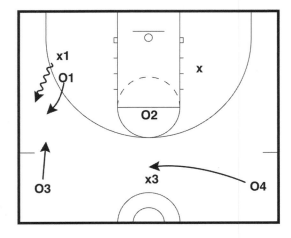

Diagram 225

Four-on-four: hatchet-man

Here we have a four-on-four alignment which brings in the alignment and movement already practiced. The emphasis for the front line is to keep the ball out of the middle and to look for the random trap. The second line will focus on covering the offensive middleman and trying to intercept the ball. As the ball is now coming down the left side of the court, O3 will look to randomly trap if the dribbler is out of control (diagram 225).

Breakdown drills: five-on-five full-court

We now have a full-court five-on-five situation with the final defensive player being introduced. His role is to protect the basket and not allow any layups. He must read and intercept any deep passes. If the middlemen do not do their job and O5 has to step over to cover a wing, the weakside middleman would rotate to take O5's position (diagram 226).

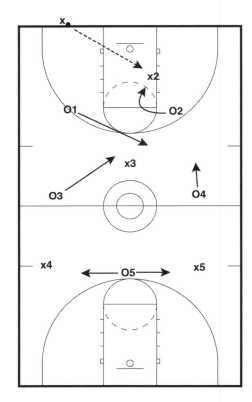

Diagram 226

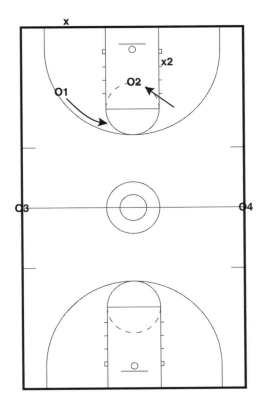

Diagram 227

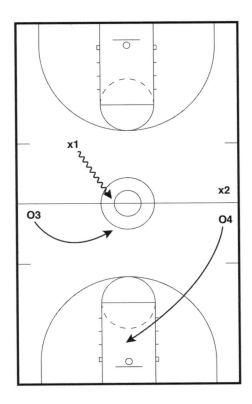

Diagram 228

Breakdown drills: full-court hatchet-man four-on-four

Player X1 will inbound to X2. O1 and O2 will play defense only to half court (diagram 227). Then O3 and O4 will pick-up X1 and X2 and play them to the other basket. O3 and O4 cannot enter the court until the ball crosses the half-court line (diagram 228).

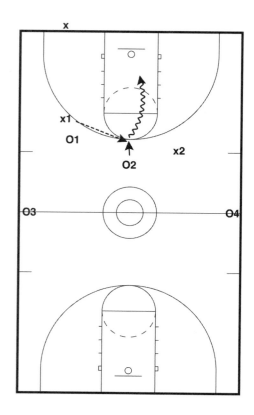

Diagram 229

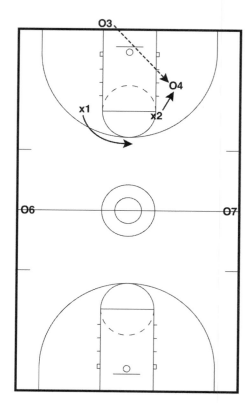

Diagram 230

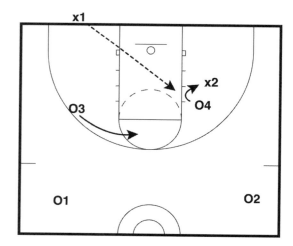

Diagram 231

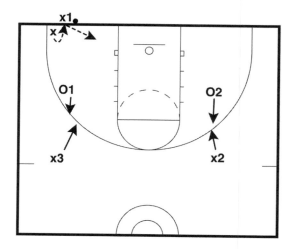

Diagram 232

If O1 or O2 intercept the ball, they immediately attack that basket. If they score, they play defense again, but only to half court. O3 and O4 will take over at half court (diagram 229). Once X1 and X2 have scored or lost possession, they will play two-on-two against O3 and O4, who must now inbound the ball. X1 and X2 will only play to the half court, where O6 and O7 will take over. This drill is continuous. It should be run eight to ten minutes each day without interruption except to make teaching points (diagram 230).

We have adjusted our defenders. Now O3 and O4 are on the front line, and we put O1 and O2 at half-court. This puts the bigger players up front (diagram 231). To give a different look, we have used O1 and O2 with their backs to the ball to try and completely "cut-off" or deny the inbound pass (diagram 232).

Some Thoughts on the 2-2-1 Zone Press

- Keep ball out of the middle. Defend half court rather than full-court.
- Look to have the front line trap. The second line should try to intercept the ball. The back line must protect.
- Force the 10-second violation.
- Cause a five-second inbound violation from your cut-off or denial defense.
- Change defenders roles, e.g., 1 and 2 take middle and 3 and 4 take front to give the defense a different look.
- Sometimes allow the entry pass. Sometimes completely deny the entry pass.
- The full-court two-versus-two-on-two hatchet-man drill is a great teaching and conditioning drill. It instructs defenders on the art of reading an offense.

Part Six:
Transition Defense

Adam Parmenter
Five-Star Basketball Camp
Mercy College, NY

Transition Defense Introduction

This chapter covers one of the most important aspects of any team's defensive repertoire—the transition game. It is all too common for a team to focus 90-100% of its practice and training time on individual and team defensive concepts geared toward the half-court game and full-court presses. The majority of points, especially at the youth and lower high school levels of basketball, are converted through fast break and transition opportunities. If you can prepare your team to minimize these scoring opportunities for your opponents, you put your team in a great position to make a conversion of your own—winning!

The following drills stress the importance of five offensive players becoming well-positioned defensive players as quickly as possible following a change of possession. Teams press, trap and pressure defensively in order to create offensive scoring opportunities. They should also prepare to quickly recover from their own mistakes or misfires in order to minimize quick and easy offensive scoring chances. A majority of layup or dunk attempts and conversions occur during a fast break situation!

If you have a great zone or half-court man-to-man defense, chances are you have faced a team whose method to defeat you is to beat you down the court. This can be effective if for any reason your defense is slow in setting up. Also, if you have a team that is used to scoring and being able to set up a press or leisurely get down the court, then a skilled team could even inbound quickly and beat you downcourt for an easy bucket.

Each of the following drills has been selected as one that would help any team work on transition defense, scramble (deficit) situations and closing out plays. They can be adjusted to your style and personnel or an upcoming opponent's style and personnel. Be creative with them, remember that every new idea in basketball is generally a conglomeration of old ideas put together in the most effective manner!

The Five-Star Fast Break Game

Fast break defense

Basketball is moving away from slowing the game down and running set plays and moving toward scoring in transition on the fast break and secondary break. Coaches should emphasize that limiting transition points is key to stopping your opponent's offense and winning games. Emphasis should be placed primarily on stopping the ball and protecting the basket.

To set up the first drill have the players make two lines at half court and the lane-line extended. The coach should stand at the center of half court with a ball. The first two players in line face the coach and do footfire. The coach will blow the whistle, and the players will sprint to the two positions (one at the top of the key to stop the ball and the other at the front of the rim to protect the ball). Then the coach will hold the ball to one side or another. On whichever side the coach holds the ball, the bottom player will come out to that wing to stop the imaginary player from receiving the ball for a layup. The top player will drop back to the rim to protect the basket. As the first players in line drop to the initial positions, the next two players in line will start footfire, and the drill will run continuously. Emphasize to the team that they need to stop the ball as soon as possible. They need to sprint to the positions. Defensive slides and backpedaling are too slow. They must communicate the entire time. Yell out who has the ball and who has the basket so two players don't sprint to the same spot. Do not give up layups. You want the offense to take the most difficult shot possible, making the offense make multiple passes which negates the fast break by allowing defensive teammates to make it down the floor.

Fast break offense instruction

In order to properly drill your defense and prepare players for game situations, you must also ensure that the offensive half of the drill is properly instructed. To set up the drill, get three lines at half court. Stand on the baseline and throw the ball to one of the three lines. Whoever gets the ball needs to dribble it down the middle of the court and jump stop at the foul line. The other two players in line fill the outside lanes running for a layup. After the player with the ball jump stops at the free-throw line, he bounce passes to one of the players running the lane for a layup and then drifts to the ball-side elbow ready to receive a pass back for a jumper. Emphasize that there should be no more than two passes in the fast break—the initial pass for a layup and the pass back to the passer for an elbow jumper. Any more passes and the defense will have gotten back and effectively stopped the fast break. Have the players first go through and make the pass for a layup, and then after a few reps make the pass back to the passer for an elbow jumper.

The offensive/defensive fast break: the game

The next progression of the drill (if time allows) is to add three players on defense. The three defensive players line up across from the offensive players with about a six-foot gap. Whichever player has the ball thrown to them, the corresponding defensive player must go back and touch half court before getting back on defense. The other two players defend the three-on-two fast break. Remember to initially emphasize what the players should be doing on offense: getting the ball to the middle of the floor, jump stopping, advancing the ball with the pass, moving to the ball-side elbow, making no more than two passes.

The drill is set up by having the offensive group line up on one sideline and the defensive group on the other sideline. Three offensive players will line up on the baseline facing the opposite basket, one under the basket and the other two players on the wings. Three defensive players will line up across from them at the free-throw line extended. To start the drill, a coach will throw a ball to one of the offensive players. The corresponding defensive player will have to run up and touch the baseline while everyone else gets downcourt on a 3-2 fast break.

The offense and defense combine to use the entire full court. The offense will play the defense full court using the fundamental principles that were taught. One group will be on offense for the first half of the drill while the second group plays defense. When it is time, the two groups will simply switch offense to defense. The length of your halves can be adjusted to the amount of time available in your practice schedule. The defensive players must:

- Sprint back to their positions (one to stop the ball at or before the top of the key, the other to protect the basket)
- The third player must sprint back to get in the play
- Communicate which spot they are going to
- Work on forcing the offense to take a jump shot and not allowing a layup
- Make the offense throw multiple passes
- Secure the rebound, not allowing second-chance points

The game goes on until the offense scores or the defense forces a turnover or secures the rebound.

The coaches will also keep score of the drill using the following scoring system:

Offense	Defense
Scoring—2 pts. (no 3-pointers)	Match up (all defensive players back 3-on-3)—1 pt.
Foul in the act of shooting—2 pts.	Any offensive turnover or rebound—1 pt.
Foul and score—3 pts.	Steal—2 pts.
Non-shooting foul—1 pt.	Blocked shot—1 pt.
Offensive rebound—1 pt.	Charge—3pts.

Points may be deducted at the coaches' discretion for various miscues such as not talking on defense, not getting the ball to the middle of the floor, etc. The points will carry over when the players switch from offense to defense. The group with the most points at the end of the two station sets wins. The losers will have to either do pushups or run suicides or something of that nature.

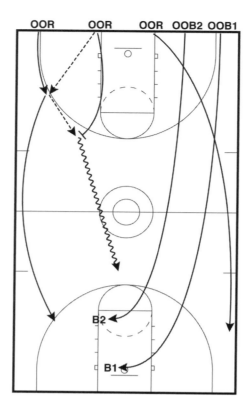

Diagram 233

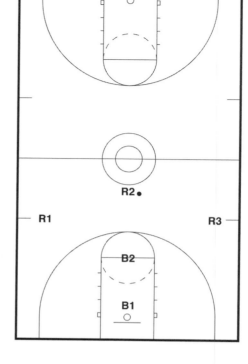

Diagram 234

Transition defense: disadvantage drill (diagram 233)

This is a full-court drill that requires communication and focuses on defensive stops in transition situations. Divide your team into two equal teams, blue and white. Start the drill with three players on offense (blue) and two players on defense (white) on the first possession. The offensive lines begin by passing from the middle to the outside then back to the middle as they move down the floor. Don't allow them to take off dribbling, as they will always beat the defense down court. The defense sprints down the floor to get into position. If the defense gains possession, they can advance up the floor and attempt to score as two offense (white) against three defense (blue). Play once down and back with each group and then start the next set of players in each group (diagram 234).

After three minutes, switch so that the white group has three offensive players and blue has two defensive players. Play for another three minutes. Keep score for each group for the total drill time. You can and should change how you keep score, but always be sure to track it to keep the drill com-

petitive. You can count made baskets, offensive or defensive rebounds, steals, deflections or defensive stops in general. Also, count double points when the offense scores or the defense gets a stop when down a player.

The drill can also be run four-on-three then three-on-four, or five-on-four then four-on-five. Players tend to love a full-court drill, not to mention the competition that this drill brings. Have a consequence for the team that did not win the drill.

Transition defense: get back drill

This is a full-court drill run in a normal five-on-five situation. Two coaches or managers are needed for this drill. One team starts on offense, the other on defense. You can run your normal motion or offensive sets looking to maximize passes and reps. The coach in the offensive zone stands out of bounds at foul-line extended without a ball. The other coach stands at half court with a ball. When the coach without the ball yells "turnover," the offense passes immediately to him and retreats on defense. The defense switches to offense and is in a transition offense situation. The coach at midcourt passes to the offense looking to score in transition. If they can't score, they set up the offense and repeat the drill. Coaches move from midcourt to the free-throw line extended. This is a defensive-minded drill, and each transition defense has to abide by the following rules:

- All defenders must sprint toward the defensive key and then initiate their defense.
- Only after touching the painted area do defenders worry about locating and stopping the ball.

- After securing the basket area, defenders close out to cover the offensive players.
- Don't allow open layups or threes; contest all shots!
- Defenders should run past the ball and their man, making sure the lane is secure before moving out to defend.
- Always backtap if caught behind the ballhandler in transition.

These are just some of the rules we play with; you can alter them to fit your defensive philosophy.

Part Seven: Defending Special Situations

Kevin Pigott
Fordham Preparatory School, NY

Out-of-Bounds Defense

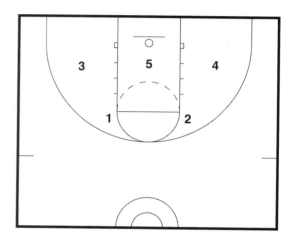

Diagram 235

As we all know, there is never enough time in our practices. There is always something that is going to suffer due to our lack of attention. The amount of time a team spends on its out-of-bound plays varies from coach to coach. Some spend an inordinate amount of time on them. These coaches are looking to get six to ten points a game off their out-of-bound plays. Others are less willing to sacrifice other parts of their practice. However, every coach must spend some time developing their out-of-bound plays.

Conversely, many teams' attention to their defensive strategies for out-of-bound plays is nothing more than an afterthought. Most teams work on this part of their game only to practice defending their own offensive plays or as part of their preparation for an opponent. It is our contention that teams should formulate and implement defensive tactics for out-of-bounds plays as part of their overall defensive strategy.

We will defend most out-of-bound plays with the 2-3 zone. We like to keep our smaller players ball-side, i.e., on the side of the inbounder (diagram 235). From this original set we can decide what defense we will go into. We always have the option to play a straight man defense if we want.

The defensive call can be made from the bench or from one of the players on the floor. Any senior on the floor can make the defensive call. Usually the players will glance over to the bench to see if the coaching staff has indicated a particular defense. The coaching staff will use their scouting reports to determine how to defend the inbounds play. The decisions are based on both the offensive set and where the offense is positioning particular players. We note, for example, where the big men are or where a shooter is located.

To Take Your Game to the Next Level: Teams will disguise their plays. Some teams will use different sets to run the same play. Some teams will use the same set to run different plays. Scouting helps in deciphering this.

To Take Your Game to the Next Level: Most communication breakdowns to defending the out-of-bounds play occur in the second half of a game. This is when your bench is farthest from the defensive baseline. From our scouting reports, we prep our kids to read the offense and then determine what defense we should be in. Ideally, they should make the call on the floor. We let our seniors call the defense, preferably one of the bigger players. Guards usually determine the offense.

We tell our players to make their own call if there is any kind of communication breakdown. We would rather have all the defenders playing the same defense—even if it is not the defense the coaching staff wants—than have four of them in the preferred defense and one of them playing a different defense.

We prefer to play man defense, however, we start in a 2-3 zone when defending the out-of-bounds play. As indicated above, there are occasions when we will defend the out-of-bounds with a man defense. The advantage of using the 2-3 zone is that it allows us to place defenders by position. It also allows us to clog the middle. From the 2-3 zone we can go into other defenses.

All of our defenses are numbered. We use two numbers for defense, e.g., 11, 12, 21, 15 and 31. Our rationale is that defensive players have two free hands to make the call. Our man defense is 11. If we were playing a straight man defense during an out-of-bounds play, we would call "11." We would signal this by holding up both hands with one finger showing one each. The first digit represents defense, so one represents man defense. The "10" series is our man defenses. The second digit represents the pick-up point of the defense, so "11" would represent a quarter-court man defense, "12" would be half-court man defense, "13" would be three-quarters court man defense, and "14" would be a full-court man defense (diagram 236). We use five to represent any special types of defense, so "15" would be our full-court match-up pressure defense.

Our 20 series is our 2-3 zone. We will usually call for a 2-3 zone as our out-of-bounds defense.

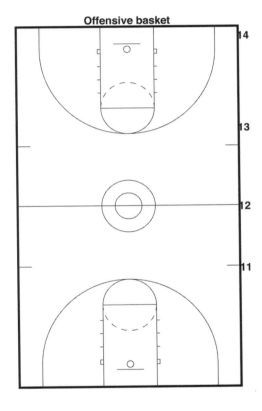

Diagram 236

Thus, to indicate a 2-3 zone with quarter-court pick-up, we would call "21." However, we add a verbal cue to indicate what defensive action occurs after the ball is inbounded. If we call "early," the defenders will match up to the offensive players before the ball is inbounded. If we call "late," the defenders will wait until the ball is either dribbled or passed outside the foul-line extended area.

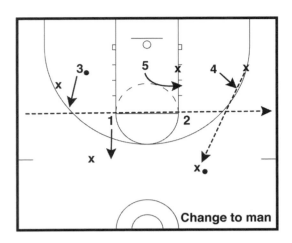

Diagram 237

Diagram 238

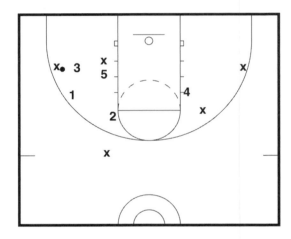

Diagram 239

Diagram 240

By calling "early," we get to keep our bigger players in the middle while still playing man defense. By calling "late," we can automatically change from zone to man when the ball is brought up high (diagram 237). This still permits us to stay in a zone defense and negate any initial screening action of the inbounds play. If the inbounds play does not score, offensive teams will bring the ball out and reorganize. "Late" allows us to change from a 2-3 zone into man when our opponent is bringing the ball outside to set up a zone offense. This changing of the defense can confuse the offense.

Many teams will run a play for the inbounder. In this case he is usually a shooter who is the recipient of a screen or two. Here we will call "special." One defender will cover the inbounder as if he were playing him in a man defense. The re-

maining four defenders will play in a box. The inbounder's defender stays with him throughout the defense possession. The other four defenders will play zone, but match up when the ball goes high as if they were playing "late" (diagram 238).

If we need to trap we will call "cover." We will trap with the wing and guard who are on the ball side (diagram 239). If we get a trap, we automatically go into man defense. When the trap occurs, the three nontrapping defenders must cover four offensive players. They must "umbrella." Each of these three defenders must cover at least two offensive players each (diagram 240).

Sometimes we will go from our 2-3 zone out-of-bounds defense into another zone. If this is the case, we want to make sure that we have the players in the right positions in order to shift into the other zone with as little chaos as possible. If we

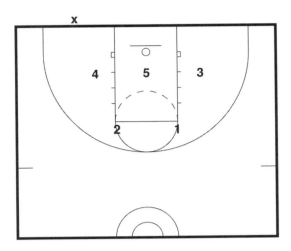

Diagram 241

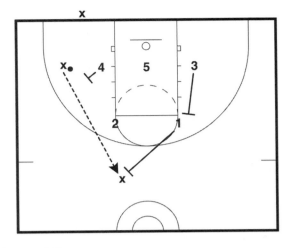

Diagram 242

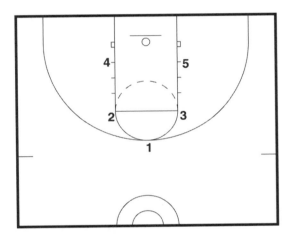

Diagram 243

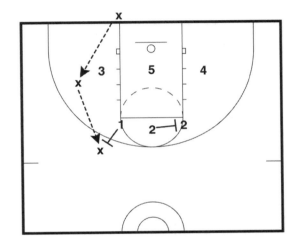

Diagram 244

want to go into our 3-2 zone, we will place our defenders differently in the 2-3. Now we will keep our bigger players on the ball side in order to get them in the right place in the 3-2 (diagram 241). We would allow the initial pass into the ball-side corner (diagram 242). Our defenders should end up where we want them in the 3-2 zone (diagram 243). The same principle would work if you wanted to get into a 1-2-2 zone.

Getting into a 1-1-3 zone is rather simple. We keep our defensive alignment with the smaller players on the ball side. The guard who plays the top of the zone must be on the ballside of the 2-3. The opposite guard must play the foul-line area. The rotation with the bottom three defenders would remain the same (diagrams 244 and 245).

You could use this with other defenses as well. What you need to do is determine where you want

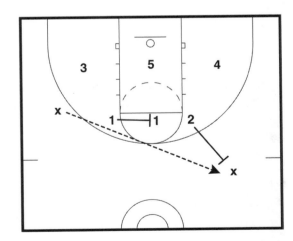

Diagram 245

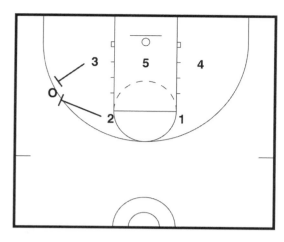

Diagram 246

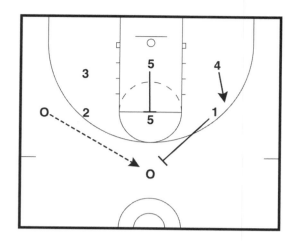

Diagram 247

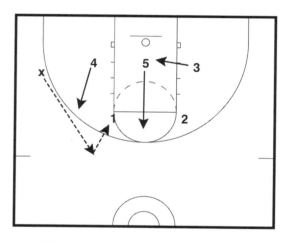

Diagram 248

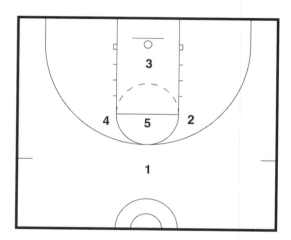

Diagram 249

To Take Your Game to the Next Level: How do you practice both executing and defending out-of-bounds plays? You can work on them at any time in your practice. Whenever you need to get into an offense, you can initiate the offense by using an out-of-bounds play or a sideline out-of-bounds play. Many of us just let the guard dribble the ball up the floor and run the offense you want to work on. Instead, by starting with an out-of-bounds play, you get an opportunity to work on them without interrupting the flow of the practice.

your defenders after the initial alignment, and what you want them to do. For example, do you want to trap out of the 1-3-1 right away, or do you want the offense to bring the ball out high? If the former, you can use "cover" and trap immediately from the 2-3 zone. If the offense breaks the trap, you can continue your pressure by switching to a 1-3-1 zone (diagrams 246, 247, and 248). Here we will use 2 and 3 as the initial trappers. If the latter, you can protect the middle with the 2-3 zone and let the offense bring the ball out. Then you can switch to the 1-3-1 zone and then trap (diagram 249). Notice how we switched the 3 and 4 positions. This allows us to get the 3 into the baseline runner position.

We normally do not play any combination defenses. However, if you wanted to switch into a combination defense, "special" would work with a box-and-one defense. I believe you could get into a triangle-and-two defense from the 2-3 zone. You would just have to decide as to which offensive players were going to get your attention.

The type of defense you will use for defending the out-of-bounds will depend upon different variables. Your scouting reports will dictate much of what you want to do. The time left on the shot clock will also be a factor. What is important is that you practice defending out-of-bounds plays as much as you practice out-of-bounds plays.

Adam Demorest
Five-Star Basketball Camp

Defense in End Game Situations

Introduction

In this section we will explore the different possibilities for playing defense in four different late-game situations: up three with less than 10 seconds left; up one or two with less than 10 seconds; a tied score with less than 10 seconds left; and down one, two, or three with 10 seconds. These types of situations come up a lot in games, and as a coach youneed to be prepared for them and prepare your teams for them. It is like the quote by John Wooden, "Failing to prepare is preparing to fail."

As with different facets of basketball, there are many different philosophies on how to guard the above mentioned situations. I hope this section better prepares you for each scenario. Furthermore, it may also reinforce or maybe change your philosophy. As with most things, there is no absolute right philosophy.

Scenario: Up by Three With Less Than 10 Seconds Remaining

Five thoughts to consider in this scenario:

1. Don't give up a three.
2. Should I play zone or man?
3. Do I double their best three-point shooter?
4. Should I foul them before they take a three-point shot?
5. Do I help on a drive to the basket?

All of the above are legitimate thoughts that come to mind when you are in this scenario. At this point ask yourself what you would do. In this case, I am going to explain my views on each and how to defend this scenario.

The first thought is probably the most basic out of the five. In this scenario, you absolutely want to protect against the three. I have heard coaches say they will let their worst shooter take it and

live with the results. I don't agree with that because I have seen some crazy things happen late in games. I prefer to look at it as an absolute: prevent any open three-point shots, no matter who is taking them.

The second thought is, "Should I play zone or man-to-man?" I think that comes down to which defensive tactic does your team use best to defend against the three-point shot. Use the one that works best for you. There is a school of thought as well about switching defenses to confuse the offensive team. I would be very careful with that, because sometimes you can outsmart yourself and confuse your team. If you are going to switch defenses, make sure you practice it often.

Do I double their best shooter? Personally, going back to thought one, I don't want to double any player in this situation, because that means somebody is going to be open to shoot the three, and I don't want to give up any uncontested shots. If you think about doing this, you will have to be able to live with the possibility of the opponent shooting an unconstested three and tying up the game.

Should I foul them before they take the three-point shot? There are many different schools of thought on this question. I would ask you to think about this: Are you willing to place somebody on the line where you can't guard them and allow them to add points to their total, stop the clock, and gamble on how the rebound may come off if they choose to miss one of the free throws? That is the reality when you put them on the line. At the program I coach with, we believe that our defense is good enough to stop the other team, and we let the defense decide the outcome—not the free-throw line.

Do I help on a drive to the basket? This has been a very hot topic lately, especially with the advent of Grinnell College's offensive system and Memphis University. Once again I go back to my first thought: no uncontested threes. So, I would not help. At the college level, there are just too many good shooters that will knock down the three as soon as you help.

Defending the scenario

Five rules to use as guideline whens defending this scenario:

1. Run a defense with no help and total denial of three-point shooters.
2. If the shooter(s) comes off picks, trail their back hip to avoid screens. Also, try to force them to curl. Third, use the defender whose man is setting the screen to show big and then get back to his man if the shooter's defender gets caught up.
3. No fouls, you don't want to stop the clock for them or give them easy points.
4. Contest any shots taken.
5. Rebound the ball.

Scenario: Up One or Two With Less than 10 Seconds Remaining

Five basic thoughts to consider in this scenario:

1. Don't give up a three.
2. Should I play zone or man?
3. Should I foul?
4. Do I help on a drive to the basket?
5. How am I going to guard the pick-and-roll?

What would you do? How would you react to each of these thoughts? The first couple of thoughts are the same as scenario one, except the emphasis on not giving up a three becomes greater in this scenario because if they hit the three, you are now down with very little or no time left.

Should I foul? I would say this depends on the situation. If a player has a layup and you can foul him without him scoring, I would foul him regardless of whether you are up one or two and make him earn that point. If the player is shooting a jump shot, I would not foul because I don't believe in fouling a jump shooter.

Do I help on a drive to the basket? Here is a very difficult situation to deal with and one you should give a lot of thought to in your preparations for defending this scenario. If you help, it will potentially open up a shot for an offensive player. If you don't help, you could potentially give up a layup. If you are only up by one, this would put you behind. If you are only up by two, this would tie the game. My thought on this situation is to stick with whatever you normally do on a drive and do not try to outsmart yourself or your players. I find players are much more comfortable doing things in a game that they have been well-trained to do in practice. So in this scenario we would help outside-in, but not inside-out. This means our guards would help, but not our posts.

How are you going to guard the pick-and-roll? This is another very difficult situation to defend and must be given a lot of thought and attention. In today's game many teams like to attack with the pick-and-roll, especially late in games as in scenario two. I think you must be able to guard the pick-and-roll several different ways depending on the offensive players running it: up and under, shimmy through, trap, jam and hedge-and-recover. We would run one of our five defensive schemes listed above for the pick-and-roll. This is dependent on the team we are playing. However, we still would emphasize no fouls, unless they were going to get a layup. Finally, we would also contest any shots.

Defending the scenario

Six rules to use as guidelines when defending this scenario:

1. Run a defense that takes away three-point shots.
2. If the shooter(s) comes off picks, trail their back hip to avoid screens. Also, try to force them to curl. Finally, use the defender whose man is setting the screen to show big and then get back to his man if the shooter's defender gets caught up.
3. No fouls, unless the offensive player has a layup and you can make sure they won't make it.
4. Have a plan in place for how you are going to defend a pick-and-roll situation.
5. Contest any shots taken.
6. Rebound the ball.

Scenario: Score is Tied With 10 Seconds Remaining

Six basic thoughts to consider in this scenario:

1. Am I more confident in my defense's or my offense's ability to win the game?

2. Don't give up a three.

3. Should I play zone or man?

4. Should I foul?

5. Do I help on a drive to the basket?

6. How am I going to guard the pick-and-roll?

What would you do? This scenario is probably the easiest of the four I am presenting in this section. I think you will find how you answer the first question is going to dictate how you will choose to defend your opponent. Think about your answer to the first question right now. When you are finished with this section, you decide how you would guard it and see if my statement above is correct.

My answer to the first question is to go to my defense. Every day we preach that defense wins championships. We believe it, which is why we work on it every day. We have the confidence that we can stop a team when we have to. I do know some coaches who will elect to foul and get the ball back on the offensive side and try and win that way. Which way are you?

Thoughts two through six are the same as in scenario two. The biggest thing to remember is that the game is tied, so we just need a stop. We would use the same schemes we had used all game long that we had practiced each day. What we don't want to do is gamble and open up the floor.

Defending the scenario

Six rules to use as guidelines when defending this scenario:

1. Run a defense that you have already successfully used to stop your opponent during the game.

2. If the shooter(s) comes off picks, trail their back hip to avoid screens and try to force them to curl. Then use the defender whose man is setting the screen to show big and then get back to his man if the shooter's defender gets caught up.

3. No fouls, unless the offensive player has a layup and you can make sure they won't make it. (If you want the ball back and are willing to foul, then you would want to foul their worst free-throw shooter as quickly as possible.)

4. Have a plan in place for how you are going to defend a pick-and-roll situation.

5. Contest any shots taken.

6. Rebound the ball.

Scenario: Down One, Two or Three With 10 Seconds Remaining

Three basic thoughts to consider in this scenario:

1. Get a turnover immediately.

2. If no turnover, then foul immediately.

3. Should I play zone or man?

What would you do? How would you react to each of these thoughts?

As you can tell by the first two thoughts in this scenario, there's a sense of urgency, because there isn't much time left and you have to get the ball back and score. I strongly suggest you have a defensive scheme that you work on every day for this situation so your players get comfortable with it and know exactly what to do under pressure. In this scenario, players don't have the time to think, so they must be able to react to the situation quickly.

I will start with thought three first: "Should I play zone or man?" My answer is to play the one that allows you to have the best chance of creating a turnover. We would either run our man-to-man and trap the first pass and cheat our help-side wing over to gamble in the passing lane for the next pass, or we would run our 1-3-1 trap and gamble for a pass. Either way we would be going for an immediate steal on the next pass. If we did not get it, we would foul immediately, regardless of who had the ball.

Defending the scenario

Three rules to use as guidelines when defending this scenario.

1. Must play aggressively and create a turnover.

2. Must foul immediately if thought one doesn't happen. Make sure to not pick up an intentional foul.

3. Don't panic.

Part Eight: Combination and Changing Defenses

Al Barbosa
LaSalle Academy, NY

Triangle-and-Two Defense

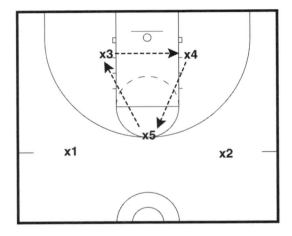

Diagram 250

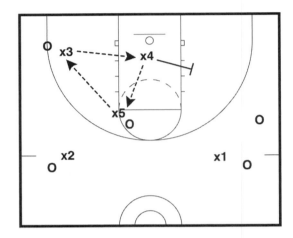

Diagram 251

Introduction

LaSalle Academy is a school rich in tradition; this can even be seen on the basketball court. The history of the triangle-and-two goes all way the back to Hall of Fame Coach Dan Buckley, and it was used by Bill Aberer when he coached LaSalle to an NYC AA championship with NBA All-Star Ron Artest. When it's appropriate, we still use this defensive strategy today.

Dan Buckley created this defense with a couple of thoughts in mind. It is designed to defend teams with one or two scorers. It was also conceived as a change-of-pace defense. This defense is certainly helped by having a quick and tall center. He does not have to be a great rebounder; however, he must be a great shot blocker, someone who will intimidate the shooters. The triangle-and-two makes it difficult for the offense to get penetration. The triangle of this defense has to be elastic. It has to move as the ball moves. This defense is designed to take away the offense's normal shot as well as its ability to drive to the basket.

Positions

There are various ways to use the two defenders outside the triangle. In most instances, however, we will play the three defenders in the triangle the same way. We will put our big man on the point of the triangle. Then we will place two good rebounders underneath the basket (diagram 250). X5 always fronts the high post on the ball side. The help-side rebounder moves toward the ball, never going past the middle of the court. Some coaches describe this point as the ball-side/help-side line. In this position the help-side rebounder can jump out and defend the weak-side offensive man in case of a quick ball reversal to the opposite side of the court (diagram 251).

Defending the Shooter

If your opponent has one outside offensive threat, we use the triangle-and-one-and-one. We attempt to double-team the shooter whenever he gets the ball (diagram 252). Another way to defend the shooter is to have one defender deny the shooter while another defender plays close

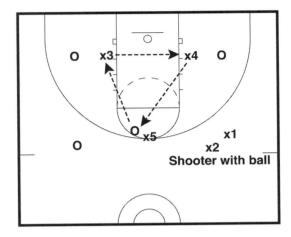

Diagram 252

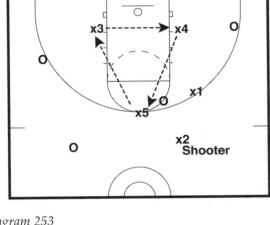

Diagram 253

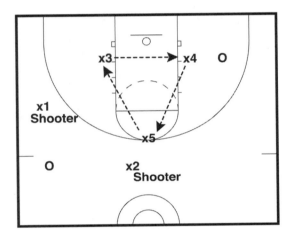

Diagram 254

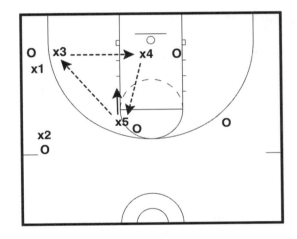

Diagram 255

enough to back up his teammate in case the shooter does catch the ball (diagram 253).

Defending Two Shooters

If the offense has two shooters, we will then cover them with two defenders playing man defense with the triangle acting as help defense.

Trapping

You can trap with your two-man defenders. You must designate certain offensive players to trap, certain offensive situations to trap, or certain areas (diagram 254). You can trap with one of your man defenders and one of your zone defenders. A great place to trap is the corner (diagram 255).

Considerations

The triangle-and-two is effective in defending the pick-and-roll. Inherently it provides help-side defense. It negates motion and screening games.

The triangle-and-two provides excellent rebounding opportunities. It even allows us to focus on boxing out offensive rebound threats with our two man defenders. Coach Buckley would emphasize the importance of "feinting" or faking the offense. This is similar to "stunting." Faking a trap causes turnovers.

The triangle-and-two struggles against teams with three or more offensive threats. You might want to switch to man defense, a match-up defense, or even an inverted triangle-and-two. We can play an inverted triangle-and-two with our

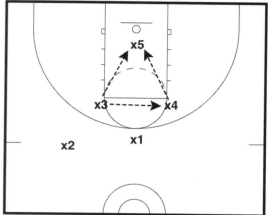

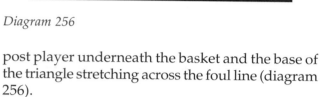

Diagram 256

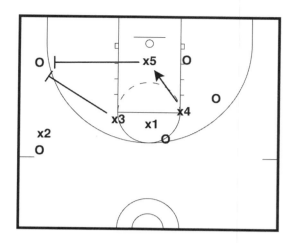

Diagram 257

post player underneath the basket and the base of the triangle stretching across the foul line (diagram 256).

The inverted triangle-and-two has some similarities to the 1-3-1 defense. The elbow defenders must cover the wings. When the ball is in the corner, it is covered by either the wing or post. The opposite elbow must drop when he becomes a help-side defender (diagram 257).

Most teams do not have an answer to the triangle-and-two. Offenses rarely prepare for it. Most coaches do not know how to attack it. Imagine running this defense with Ron Artest.

Adam Parmenter
Five-Star Basketball Camp
Mercy College, NY

Changing Defenses

Introduction

In recent years, a few prominent college teams have shown to be successful at changing defenses not only throughout a series of possessions and games, but even during a possession. This changing pattern of defenses, if concealed and not easily timed, can be particularly effective against teams that run a variety of set plays. This section focuses on switching defenses within possessions.

Here is an example: Team A runs a set of plays designed to screen a zone and create scoring opportunities. If Team B shows a 2-3 zone and uses Team A's play call as a signal to match up, they effectively can counteract the set play. Although some zone sets can be effective versus man-to-man, this normally is not the case, and unless instructed to do so in pre-game scouting, players may not be prepared to react.

Switching Within Possessions

Switching from zone to man

There are various ways and effective methods in switching from a zone set to a man-to-man defense within a possession. Above, we discussed switching from a 2-3 zone to a man set. The signal to break the zone in favor of man is the offensive team's play call versus the zone. This can be useful, as generally a play is called with a guard pulling the ball out and setting up an offense. The defense can match up and sit within their zones until the offense initiates, at which point the offense is running and quickly realizing the zone defense is no longer staying in their zones!

Switches can be timed; however, the odds of the switch coming at a disadvantageous moment are too high for this author to suggest that method. If you tell the defense to switch to man at 15 seconds on the shot clock, and 15 seconds comes as the offense has made a penetrating pass to the foul line or short corner or other interior area, the defense is liable to match up and be late in guarding a slashing offensive player. For this reason, be certain that your players are trained in matching up from the inside out, meaning that they locate open players on the interior before the exterior. Or you can build in certain areas where the zone does not switch to man if the offense has possession in those areas. So if an offensive-player dribble penetrates to the foul line, your zone collapses accordingly and denies interior passes, rather than matching up to perimeter players and leaving holes in the interior!

Switching from zone to zone

If your opponent has a specific patterned offense versus your zone, you could use either a pattern of ball movement or a certain player movement to indicate a change in your zone. The most common version of this concept would be a 3-2 zone switching to a 2-3 zone. There are two ways you could pull this off, and if you have a larger, potentially slower center, you may not want him having the responsibility of guarding the corner, and an offense may be looking to exploit this situation.

Option 1

As the ball goes to the corner opposite your post player, the wing defender on the weak side peals down and becomes the baseline defender in a 2-3 zone. Thus, if the ball is reversed, that player now has the responsibility of defending the corner.

Option 2

If the ball goes to the corner on the side of your post player, the wing defender moves down with the pass and maintains this position in a 2-3 zone set.

Other options

Try switching from a 2-3 zone to a box-and-one when a team's star scorer catches in a certain position. Be sure that your best defender is positioned to defend him in that position. Drop the others to cover.

In Closing

If you trap within your zone defense, you technically already run a switching defense since your zone is basically changing to a triangle-and-two, with the two defenders in a trapping situation. If your players work well with this change, chances are they will be able to handle the switching action of these zone looks. You can also be creative with this, but keep in mind that the more complex they are, the harder the defensive changes will be to execute. Also, verbal cues are great but are not necessarily consistent, as what you call during a practice session may not be heard during a game situation, especially on the road! Work on verbal cues from opposing point guards, ball position on the floor, or a specific time with designated dead areas in order to initiate your defensive change.

As with any defense, you must drill, drill, drill these concepts into your players' minds, as well as any specific changes for upcoming opponents. You can utilize shell offenses or live game situations to achieve these points. Be sure to go over any dead areas and reinforce these within your drill work.

Index by Contributor

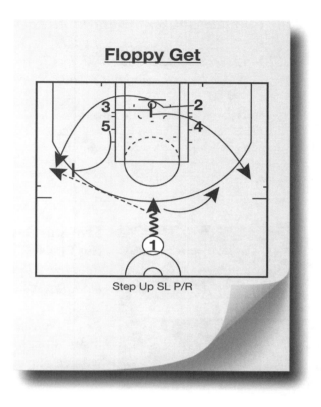

Five-Star Basketball Presents My Favorite Moves: Shooting Like the Stars
Featuring Chamique Holdsclaw and Tina Thompson with Nikki McCray, Coco Miller, Ukari Figgs and Stephanie White

ISBN-13: 9781930546585 • $12.95 128 pages • b/w illustrations throughout • trade paper

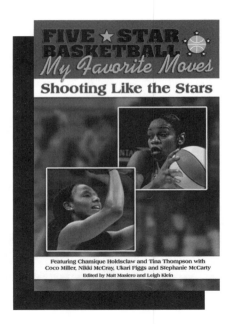

"Written by coaches, these titles are good additions to any sports collection. They give advice on how to succeed in the game, regardless of gender. In each book, six professional female athletes are featured, highlighting the players' specific abilities and offering drills for readers to work on." — *School Library Journal*

Five-Star Basketball Presents My Favorite Moves: Making the Big Plays
Featuring Tamika Catchings and Mwadi Mabika with Katie Douglas, Kelly Miller, Nykesha Sales and Kristin Folkl

Five-Star Basketball, the long-time leader in basketball instruction, has teamed up with six of the greatest professional women players to bring young players everywhere a state-of-the-art drill book like no other.

ISBN-13: 9781930546592 • $12.95 128 pages • b/w illustrations throughout • trade paper

Five-Star Basketball Coaches' Playbook
Edited by Leigh Klein and Matt Masiero

More than 320 Five-Star campers have played at least one game in the NBA; including the following: Michael Jordan, Jerry Stackhouse, Stevie Francis, Vince Carter, Sam Cassell, Zach Randolph, Rasheed Wallace, Jamal Mashburn, Alonzo Mourning, Grant Hill, Stephon Marbury, Isiah Thomas, Patrick Ewing, Moses Malone and Lebron James.

ISBN-13:9781930546714 • $18.95 256 pages • photos & diagrams trade paper

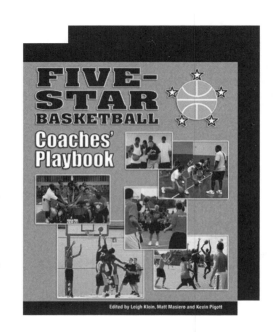

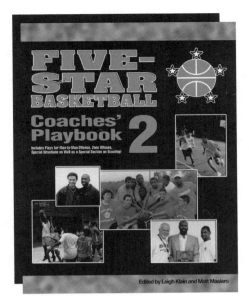

Five-Star Basketball Coaches' Playbook, Volume 2
Edited by Leigh Klein and Matt Masiero

The follow-up volume to the popular 2004 playbook, *Five-Star Basketball Coaches' Playbook* includes new plays from even more coaches who have made Five-Star Basketball Camps the premier basketball training ground in the country. This volume also includes a section on scouting.

ISBN-13:9781930546806 • $18.95 280 pages • photos & diagrams trade paper

Five-Star Girls' Basketball Drills, 2nd Edition
Edited by Stephanie Gaitley, Leigh Klein and Matt Masiero

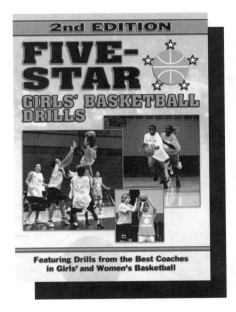

Five-Star Basketball Camps have long been synonymous with quality basketball instruction -- some of the best players in the world have been Five-Star campers: including Michael, Patrick, Isaiah, Moses, Christian, Alonzo, Grant, Stephon, The Rainman, Elton, Allan, Jayson and Vince! In 1999 eight former Five-Star Campers were selected as NBA first round draft picks: Elton Brand, Steve Francis, Richard Hamilton, Ron Artest, Trajan Langdon, Dion Glover, Corey Maggette and Jumaine Jones!

As a longtime leader in basketball instruction, Five-Star feels it must continue in its quest to educate young players about their sport. About 20 years ago, Five-Star published a book based on the drills and teachings of their boys' camps Five-Star Basketball Drills, that has become an essential part of every coach's library. In 2000, Five-Star compiled and produced the most comprehensive, state-of-the-art collection of drills by girls' and women's coaches ever assembled. In 2003, we put together this updated version of *Five-Star Girls' Basketball Drills* with more of what was loved in the first edition: more great drills, more great coaches, more information on how to make the most of your playing time as a player and how to get the most out of your team if you are a coach!

*ISBN-13: 9781930546608 • $16.95 •320 pages
more than 200 diagrams • trade paper*